SUNDAY DISMISSALS FOR THE RCIA

Sunday Dismissals for the RCIA

Mary K. Milne, O.S.U.

Foreword by
Maria Marek, I.W.B.S.

A Liturgical Press Book

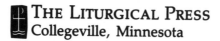
THE LITURGICAL PRESS
Collegeville, Minnesota

Cover design by Greg Becker

The dismissals presented in this book may be photocopied without further
permission for use by parishes and communities.

2	3	4	5	6	7	8	9

Library of Congress Cataloging-in-Publication Data

Milne, Mary K., 1936–
   Sunday dismissals for the RCIA / Mary K. Milne ; foreword by
Maria Marek.
     p. cm.
   ISBN 0-8146-2145-7
   1. Catholic Church. Ordo initiationis Christianae adultorum.
2. Catholic Church—Liturgy—Texts. 3. Initiation rite—Religious aspects—
Catholic Church. 4. Catholic Church—Liturgy,
Experimental. I. Title.
BX2045.I553M556 1993
264'.020813—dc20

93-28694
CIP

To my dear mother, Agnes F. Milne,
who journeyed to the Lord
during the writing of this book.

Contents

Cycle A
Advent Season

Christmas Season

Lenten Season

The Sacred Triduum

Easter Season

Ordinary Time

Cycle B
Advent Season

Christmas Season

Lenten Season

The Sacred Triduum

Easter Season

Ordinary Time

Cycle C

Advent Season

Christmas Season

Lenten Season

The Sacred Triduum

Easter Season

Ordinary Time

Appendix

Foreword

Some years ago the provisional text for the *Rite of Christian Initiation of Adults* was first published in English and in 1988 the American bishops promulgated the rite again with many pastoral adaptations for use in the United States. It has been a great joy to be involved with the pastoral implementation of the adult catechumenate over the past years, as parish teams struggle to bring to life the *Rite of Christian Initiation of Adults*. *Sunday Dismissals for the RCIA* offers a wonderful pastoral adaptation for the form of the dismissal rite. You may wish to see paragraphs #67 and #116 in the *Rite of Christian Initiation of Adults* to review the suggested dismissal ritual.

I am grateful to Mary K. Milne for writing this resource of dismissal prayers that have long been part of her experience in planning catechumenate sessions. The members of the San Antonio Archdiocesan Committee on the Catechumenate have been fortunate in her sharing her gifts in various workshops and her pastoral insight, and I was aware that she developed a model for dismissal rites based on the thematic message of the lectionary readings. She has often shared these model prayers with other team members as a way of bringing a warm hospitality and refocusing the catechumens' attention on the readings for the catechumenate session.

As the catechumenate teams begin to explore this resource they will be pleasantly surprised to find a model prayer for each Sunday and major feast of the liturgical year as well as a suggested intercession for the prayers of the faithful. She also shows great care in citing the Scripture passages which are the inspiration for each dismissal prayer. I know how often as a catechist for the catechumenate I searched for more creative and hospitable ways to dismiss catechumens. Catechists will find this a wonderful addition to their pastoral resources in helping them be more creative in the ritual aspect of the catechumenate. I hope that this text will serve as a catalyst for team members to develop their own unique styles of dismissal prayers.

Maria Marek, I.W.B.S.
Director, San Antonio Forum
on the Catechumenate

Preface

This practical book takes to heart Jim Dunning's statement, "Don't dismiss the dismissals." It addresses the knotty question of exclusion, which some individuals felt "dismissals" conveyed. The following pages offer parishes a loving way, based on the Scriptures of each Sunday, to send their candidates and catechumens from the assembled community.

With a growing understanding among Catholics that the Scriptures do touch their lives, provide nourishment and are a real source of spiritual growth, "dismissals" are beginning to be seen for what they really are: "sendings." Instead of having the uninitiated remain to watch the community partake in the Eucharistic meal, from which they are excluded, catechumens and candidates are sent to break open the Word of God in their lives, the source of their nourishment during this period of formation.

As the worshipping community sees them dismissed each week, they themselves become more aware of who their candidates and catechumens are. They hear the presider set the tone for each session, and a hunger for the Eucharist is gradually built up within the uninitiated as they often hear that their parish family looks forward to the day when they will join them at the Eucharistic table.

Through the weekly dismissals the candidates and catechumens actually experience a sense of belonging to a genuine community, a community which cares enough to see that they are nourished weekly through further reflections on the Scripture readings of the day. They are not spectators now, but participators, actively engaged with the Word of God.

In the parish where I spent much of my time working with the adult catechumenate, many of our parishioners really felt like they knew our candidates and catechumens. Parishioners saw them process out to reflect on the Word of God Sunday after Sunday for an entire liturgical year, and they often heard them called by name. So when shopping or dining, it was not unusual for parishioners to approach one of them and introduce themselves. And what a joy it was for these catechumens to feel that they belonged, that people truly cared about them.

Dismissals can provide parishioners with a wonderful opportunity to become involved in welcoming new members into the parish family. As the community gathers each Sunday, they begin to look for the uninitiated and miss them when they are not present. A sense of pride develops when parishioners consider that people want to join with them, embracing God in our Catholic tradition. Dismissals have a tremendous witness value to cradle Catholics!

So, don't dismiss the dismissals; they send the uninitiated not *from* but *to* Christ's presence—in his Word. In using them you will come to see their value in the entire process of initiating new members into our faith community.

It is my hope that the presider will become so comfortable with the format provided here that he will eventually be freed from these pages and speak to the uninitiated from his heart. This book is a model; it is a springboard for offering hospitality to our candidates and catechumens.

I wish to acknowledge the assistance of Rev. Charles H. Miller, S.M., in proofreading the manuscript and to express my gratitude for the many hours he spent at the computer helping me meet my deadline.

Mary K. Milne, O.S.U.

First Sunday of Advent (A)

[After the proclamation of the gospel or after the homily, the presider says:]

> **Would our candidates and catechumens please come forward?**

[When they have reached the dismissal area, he walks over to them and dismisses them with these words:]

> **My dear candidates and catechumens,**
> > **we welcome you into the rich Advent traditions**
> > > **of your Catholic faith community**
> > **as we begin a new liturgical year this morning.**
> **This Advent season opens with a summons to**
> > **watchfulness.**
> > **The Lord, who came as our brother in the flesh,**
> > **continues to come into our lives. . . .**
> > **You will recognize him if you are watchful.**
> **May each of you experience his light**
> > **and be open to the birth of new possibilities**
> > **as you continue your journey**
> > > **into the fullness of our Catholic faith.**
>
> **Go now in the peace of Christ to reflect**
> > **on today's Scriptures.**
> **We look forward to the day**
> > **when you will gather with us**
> > **around the Eucharistic table.**

Prayer of the faithful:

> **That our candidates and catechumens may become more aware of the presence of Christ in their daily lives, let us pray to the Lord.**

Dismissal based on Isa 2:1-5; Matt 24:37-44.

Second Sunday of Advent (A)

[After the proclamation of the gospel or after the homily, the presider says:]

>   **Would our candidates and catechumens please come forward?**

[When they have reached the dismissal area, he walks over to them and dismisses them with these words:]

>   **My dear candidates and catechumens,**
>   **Advent challenges each of us with the prophet's call**
>   **to prepare the way of the Lord**
>   **and to make straight his path into our hearts**
>   **and into our world.**
>   **May all our complacency give way to conversion**
>   **and our efforts during Advent be those of**
>   **peacemakers.**
>
>   **Go now in the peace of Christ**
>   **and be nourished by the Scriptures**
>   **which have been proclaimed this day.**
>   **We long for the day when you will gather with us**
>   **to be nourished at the Eucharistic table.**

Prayer of the faithful:

>   **That our candidates and catechumens may accept the challenge of the Scriptures in their lives, let us pray to the Lord.**

Dismissal based on Rom 15:4-9; Matt 3:1-12.

Third Sunday of Advent (A)

[After the proclamation of the gospel or after the homily, the presider says:]

Would our candidates and catechumens please come forward?

[When they have reached the dismissal area, he walks over to them and dismisses them with these words:]

**My dear candidates and catechumens,
   may the God of glory and splendor
      at whose touch the wilderness blossoms,
      broken lives are made whole,
      and frightened hearts find courage,
   open your eyes to his hidden presence
      and loosen your tongues
      in truth, gentleness, and compassion.
May God grant each of you perseverance
      and patience
   during this Advent time of longing and
      expectation.**

**Go now in the peace of Christ
   and be nourished by the Word of God
   we have shared this morning.
We look forward to the day
   when you will also gather with us
   at the Eucharistic table.**

Prayer of the faithful:

**That our candidates and catechumens may experience
the hidden presence of the Lord in their lives during
this Advent season, let us pray to the Lord.**

Dismissal based on Isa 35:1-6, 10; Jas 5:7-10; Matt 11:2-11.

Fourth Sunday of Advent (A)

[After the proclamation of the gospel or after the homily, the presider says:]

> Would our candidates and catechumens please come forward?

[When they have reached the dismissal area, he walks over to them and dismisses them with these words:]

> My dear candidates and catechumens,
>> in the psalms of David,
>> in the words of the prophets,
>> and in the dream of Joseph,
>>> God's promise is spoken
>>> and, at last, takes flesh in the womb of Mary.
>> May Emmanuel, God with us,
>>> find a welcome in your hearts
>>> and take flesh in your lives
>>>> as you reflect on his Word
>>>> and the meanings it brings.
>
>> Go now in the peace of Christ
>>> to reflect on the Scriptures
>>> and break open the Word of God for your lives.

Prayer of the faithful:

> That our candidates and catechumens may see the Lord's goodness and promise working in their own lives, we pray to the Lord.

Dismissal based on Isa 7:10-14; Rom 1:1-7; Matt 1:18-24.

Christmas Day (A)

[After the proclamation of the gospel or after the homily, the presider says:]

Would our candidates and catechumens please come forward?

[When they have reached the dismissal area, he walks over to them and dismisses them with these words:]

My dear candidates and catechumens,
  we wish you the joy of this day!
May your reflections on the good news
  just proclaimed in our midst
    deepen your conviction
    that light overcomes darkness,
    and that each of you is called
      to experience his *enduring love*.

Go now to be nourished by the Word of God,
  his gift to us.
We long for the day when you will also be
  nourished
  at the Eucharistic table.

Prayer of the faithful:

May our candidates and catechumens experience the enduring love of the Lord in their lives, let us pray to the Lord.

Dismissal based on John 1:1-18.

Holy Family (A)

[After the proclamation of the gospel or after the homily, the presider says:]

> **Would our candidates and catechumens please come forward?**

[When they have reached the dismissal area, he walks over to them and dismisses them with these words:]

> **My dear candidates and catechumens,**
> **today's Scripture readings,**
> **though reflecting a patriarchal family pattern,**
> **remind us that respect, reverence, and love**
> **are timeless values for family life.**
> **May your relationships within your own families**
> **be guided by the virtues presented to us**
> **by Paul today: the virtues of**
> **compassion, kindness, meekness,**
> **patience, forgiveness, and love.**
> **May the love that binds you to your families**
> **extend beyond them to those who need**
> **your patience and compassion.**
>
> **Go now in the peace of Christ to be nourished**
> **by the Scriptures we have shared today.**

Prayer of the faithful:

> **May our candidates and catechumens experience**
> **warmth and welcome from us, their parish family, let**
> **us pray to the Lord.**

Dismissal based on Col 3:12-21.

Mary, Mother of God (A)

[After the proclamation of the gospel or after the homily, the presider says:]

Would our candidates and catechumens please come forward?

[When they have reached the dismissal area, he walks over to them and dismisses them with these words:]

My dear candidates and catechumens,
  on this feast of Mary, the Mother of God,
    I pray that each of you may also experience
    the graciousness of our God.
  Like Mary, may you learn
    to treasure those times
    when God makes himself known to you
    and reflect upon his presence in your lives.

  Go now in the peace of Christ
    to ponder the Scriptures
    and break open the Word of God in your lives.

Prayer of the faithful:

That our candidates and catechumens may find in Mary, the Mother of God, a model for their own lives, let us pray to the Lord.

Dismissal based on Num 6:22-27; Luke 2:16-21.

Second Sunday after Christmas (A)

[After the proclamation of the gospel or after the homily, the presider says:]

> Would our candidates and catechumens please come forward?

[When they have reached the dismissal area, he walks over to them and dismisses them with these words:]

> My dear candidates and catechumens,
>> the Letter to the Ephesians which we have just read
>> expresses our sentiments this morning:
>> we thank God for you and pray for you,
>>> that you may know more clearly the Lord Jesus
>>> and the love that he has for you.
> May your innermost vision be so clarified
>> that you see how he is calling each of you
>> into his own likeness.
>> For that is your glorious heritage!
>
> Go now in the peace of Christ
>> to reflect on the Scripture readings
>> proclaimed in our midst and on the heritage
>>> which is yours in Christ Jesus, our Lord.

Prayer of the faithful:

> That our candidates and catechumens may experience
> in this community the wealth of their Catholic heritage
> and a sense of the hope that is theirs as they continue
> their faith journey, let us pray to the Lord.

Dismissal based on Eph 1:3-6, 15-18.

Epiphany (A)

[After the proclamation of the gospel or after the homily, the presider says:]

Would our candidates and catechumens please come forward?

[When they have reached the dismissal area, he walks over to them and dismisses them with these words:]

My dear candidates and catechumens,
   today we celebrate the feast of Epiphany,
      the manifestation of Christ to all peoples.
In the journey of the kings, we recall our own journey
      as the same Lord leads us out of darkness
      and even accompanies us along the way.
Our prayer is for you to persevere in your faith journey,
      to be open and ready to offer your gifts to God.

Go now in the peace of Christ
      to reflect on the Scriptures
      and be nourished on the Word of God.
We look forward to the day when your journey
      will bring you to the Eucharistic table.

Prayer of the faithful:

That our candidates and catechumens may find our parish family a light to them on their journey into the fullness of our faith community, let us pray to the Lord.

Dismissal based on Matt 2:1-12.

Baptism of the Lord (A)

[After the proclamation of the gospel or after the homily, the presider says:]

> **Would our candidates and catechumens please come forward?**

[When they have reached the dismissal area, he walks over to them and dismisses them with these words:]

> **My dear candidates and catechumens,**
> > **just as John the Baptist caught sight of Jesus**
> > > **coming toward him,**
> >
> > **may each of you be aware of the Lord**
> > > **as he approaches you throughout the week.**
> >
> > **Let him open your eyes to see just how you can**
> > > **heal the sick and lonely,**
> > > **reach out to the poor,**
> > > **and challenge evil in all its forms.**
>
> **Go now in the peace of Christ**
> > **to reflect on the Scriptures**
> > **and break open the Word of God in your lives.**

Prayer of the faithful:

> **That our candidates and catechumens may recognize the Lord in the sick, the lonely, the poor and oppressed, and that they may respond with the Lord's compassion and love, let us pray to the Lord.**

Dismissal based on Isa 42:1-4, 6-7; Matt 3:13-17.

First Sunday of Lent (A)

[At the end of the Rite of Sending, the presider addresses the following words to the candidates and catechumens as their dismissal:]

> **And so, my dear Elect,**
>> **in the name of this parish family, I now send you**
>> (Names of the Elect are inserted here.)
>> **to your cathedral this evening**
>>> **to be joined by other catechumens who are seeking**
>>> **baptism in our faith,**
>>> **and other candidates who are seeking**
>>>> **full communion in the Catholic community.**
>
> [The presider extends his hands over the Elect]
>> **You have been chosen by God**
>>> **and have entered with us into this way of Lent.**
>> **May Christ Jesus himself**
>>> **teach you the value of prayer and fasting**
>>>> **in meeting temptation,**
>>>> **especially during this time of Lenten retreat.**
>
> **Go in peace, soon you will gather with us**
>> **to be nourished at the Eucharistic table.**

Prayer of the faithful:

> **That all candidates and catechumens may experience the universality and love of our Catholic faith tradition as they meet with the bishop for the Rite of Election.**

Dismissal based on Matt 4:1-11.

Optional Dismissal for First Sunday of Lent (A)

(To be used when the Rite of Sending does not take place.)

[After the proclamation of the gospel or after the homily, the presider says:]

> **Would our candidates and catechumens please come forward?**

[When they have reached the dismissal area, he walks over to them and dismisses them with these words:]

> **My dear candidates and catechumens,**
> **you gather with us today as we begin the season of Lent.**
> **With Jesus each of us is led into the desert**
> **to be liberated from the compulsions of the world**
> **and to open our hearts to the kingdom of God.**
> **We invite you to join with us**
> **in prayer,**
> **in fasting,**
> **and in almsgiving,**
> **three ways through which God**
> **makes his presence known to us.**
>
> **Go now in the peace of Christ**
> **to reflect on the Scriptures**
> **and break open the Word of God in your lives.**

Prayer of the faithful:

> **That our candidates and catechumens may enter wholeheartedly into the grace-filled season of Lent to be liberated from the compulsions of our world and be open to the inspirations of the Spirit, let us pray to the Lord.**

Dismissal based on theme of the Lenten season.

Second Sunday of Lent (A)

[After the proclamation of the gospel or after the homily, the presider says:]

Would our Elect please come forward?

[When they have reached the dismissal area, he walks over to them and dismisses them with these words:]

My dear Elect,
may the light of the transfigured Jesus
shine upon each of you:
relieve you from any fear,
any holding back in your Lenten journey.
O Lord, open our Elect to hear your voice
and the inspirations you give them.
Transform these your chosen ones
into the likeness of your Son, Jesus.

Go now, my dear Elect, in the peace of Christ
to be nourished on the Word of God
as you continue your journey with us
through the grace-filled season of Lent.

Prayer of the faithful:

For our Elect, that they may be open to the ways in which Jesus wishes to transform their lives, let us pray to the Lord.

Dismissal based on Matt 17:1-9.

Optional Dismissal for Second Sunday of Lent (A)

(To be used when there are no Elect.)

[After the proclamation of the gospel or after the homily, the presider says:]

> **Would our candidates and catechumens please come forward?**

[When they have reached the dismissal area, he walks over to them and dismisses them with these words:]

> **My dear candidates and catechumens,**
> **may the light of the transfigured Lord**
> **shine upon each of you**
> **and relieve you of any fear or holding back**
> **during this grace-filled season.**
> **May you be transformed into the likeness of Jesus**
> **as you continue your Lenten work with us.**
>
> **Go now in the peace of Christ**
> **to be nourished by the Word of God**
> **which will sustain you on your journey.**

Prayer of the faithful:

> **For our candidates and catechumens, that they may be open to the ways in which Jesus wishes to transform their lives, let us pray to the Lord.**

Dismissal based on Matt 17:1-9.

Third Sunday of Lent (A)

[At the end of the First Scrutiny the presider addresses the Elect:]

My dear Elect,
your experience and our experience
has been that of the Samaritan woman.
Now may we seek from Jesus
living water:
a water which will help us see ourselves
for who we really are,
a water which will satisfy our deepest longings.
We send you forth to reflect on your experience
and continue to be nourished by the Word of God.

Go now in the peace of Christ.
we eagerly await the day when you will gather
with us
at the Eucharistic banquet.

Prayer of the faithful:

That our Elect may experience Jesus as the "living
water," refreshing them throughout their faith
journey, let us pray to the Lord.

Dismissal based on John 4:5-42.

Optional Dismissal for Third Sunday of Lent (A)

(To be used when there are no Elect.)

[After the proclamation of the gospel or after the homily, the presider says:]

> **Would our candidates and catechumens please come forward?**

[When they have reached the dismissal area, he walks over to them and dismisses them with these words:]

> **My dear candidates and catechumens,**
>> **let us join the Samaritan at the well**
>>> **and seek from Jesus living water:**
>>> **a water which will help us see ourselves**
>>>> **for who we really are,**
>>> **a water which will satisfy our deepest longings**
>>>> **and bring us peace.**
>
>> **Go now in the peace of Christ**
>>> **to be nourished by the Word of God,**
>>> **living water, which is ours for the taking.**

Prayer of the faithful:

> **That our candidates and catechumens may experience Jesus as "living water," refreshment on their journey, let us pray to the Lord.**

Dismissal based John 4:5-42.

Fourth Sunday of Lent (A)

[At the end of the Second Scrutiny, the presider addresses the Elect:]

> **And now, my dear Elect,**
> > **until we meet again at the next scrutiny,**
> > > **go in peace,**
> > > **and may he who is the Light of the World**
> > > **be with each of you.**
>
> > **We send you forth to reflect on the account**
> > > **of the man born blind,**
> > > **and how that person is you.**
> > **May you be nourished by the Word of God**
> > > **made present in your lives.**
> > **Your whole parish family longs to have you gather**
> > > **with us**
> > > **at the banquet of the Eucharist.**

Prayer of the faithful:

> **For our Elect, that they may truly experience the Lord opening their eyes to a Christian vision of the world, let us pray to the Lord.**

Dismissal based on John 9:1-41.

Optional Dismissal for Fourth Sunday of Lent (A)

(To be used when there are no Elect.)

[After the proclamation of the gospel or after the homily, the presider says:]

> **Would our candidates and catechumens please come forward?**

[When they have reached the dismissal area, he walks over to them and dismisses them with these words:]

> **My dear candidates and catechumens,**
> > **today a man blind from birth is confronted**
> > > **by the Light of the World,**
> > > > **but it doesn't seem to make his immediate**
> > > > **world any easier.**
> > **Amazingly, those who say they can see**
> > > **are certainly the blind ones in this account.**
> > **Perhaps we need to ask ourselves**
> > > **how faithful our vision is. . . .**
> > **May each of you experience Jesus**
> > > **as a light in your life**
> > > > **helping you to see the real obstacles**
> > > > **in your faith journey.**
>
> > **Go now in the peace of Christ**
> > > **to ponder the Scriptures**
> > > **and break open the Word of God in your lives.**

Prayer of the faithful:

> **For our candidates and catechumens, that they may truly seek to live by a Christian vision of the world, let us pray to the Lord.**

Dismissal based on John 9:1-41.

Fifth Sunday of Lent (A)

[At the end of the Third Scrutiny the presider addresses the Elect:]

> My dear friends,
>> the Lord Jesus raised Lazarus from the dead
>>> as a sign that he had come
>>> to give us life in full measure.
>> May he rescue you, our Elect,
>>> from all death-dealing situations
>>> as you seek life in the sacraments.
>> By his Holy Spirit,
>>> may he fill each of you with new life,
>>> increasing your faith, hope, and love,
>>> so that you may have life to the fullest
>>>> and thus come to share in his resurrection.
>
> My dear Elect,
>> we now send you forth to reflect more deeply
>> upon the Word of God
>> and the events which we have shared today.

Prayer of the faithful:

> For our Elect, that they may learn to trust in the Lord and his power in the death-dealing situations of their own lives, let us pray to the Lord.

Dismissal based on John 11:1-45.

Optional Dismissal for Fifth Sunday of Lent (A)
(To be used when there are no Elect.)

[After the proclamation of the gospel or after the homily, the presider says:]

> **Would our candidates and catechumens please come forward?**

[When they have reached the dismissal area, he walks over to them and dismisses them with these words:]

> **My dear candidates and catechumens,**
> > **the Lord raised Lazarus from the dead**
> > > **as a sign that he had come**
> > > **to give us life in full measure.**
> > **May each of you learn to trust the Lord**
> > > **to also liberate you**
> > > **from the death-dealing situations**
> > > > **of your lives.**
>
> > **Go now in the peace of Christ**
> > > **to reflect on the Scriptures**
> > > **and break open the Word of God in your lives.**

Prayer of the faithful:

> **That our candidates and catechumens may come to rely on the Lord in the death-dealing situations of their own lives, let us pray to the Lord.**

Dismissal based on John 11:1-45.

Passion/Palm Sunday (A)

[After the proclamation of the gospel or after the homily, the presider says:]

Would our Elect please come forward?

[When they have reached the dismissal area, he walks over to them and dismisses them with these words:]

My dear Elect,
you join with us today to begin
the most solemn week of the year.
Holy Mother Church extends to each of you
the many graces and blessings of this holy week.

I ask that you now continue your preparation
by reflecting on God's Word:
consider Christ's attitude,
pray that his attitude becomes more your own.

Go forth now to be nourished by the Scriptures.
We look forward to your joining with us
as we celebrate Holy Thursday and Good Friday.
We, too, long for the Holy Saturday Vigil,
when you will celebrate with us in fullness.

Prayer of the faithful:

For our Elect as they begin their final preparations for
baptism and full communion with this Catholic faith
community at the Easter Vigil, let us pray to the Lord.

Dismissal based on Phil 2:6-11.

Optional Dismissal Passion/Palm Sunday (A)

(To be used when there are no Elect.)

[After the proclamation of the gospel or after the homily, the presider says:]

> Would our candidates and catechumens please come forward?

[When they have reached the dismissal area, he walks over to them and dismisses them with these words:]

> My dear candidates and catechumens,
>> Jesus identifies himself with us
>>> through his death on the cross.
>> He willingly faces the greatest of our fears—
>>> annihilation.
>
> He has identified himself with us,
>> now it is up to each of you
>>> to reflect
>>> on how you have identified yourself with him
>>> throughout your Lenten journey.
>
> Go now in the peace of Christ
>> to ponder the Scriptures
>> and break open the Word of God in your lives.

Prayer of the faithful:

> That through their Lenten journey, our candidates and catechumens are becoming more Christ-like, let us pray to the Lord.

Dismissal based on theme of Sunday.

Holy Thursday—Presentation of the Our Father (A)

[After the proclamation of the gospel or after the homily, the presider says:]

Would our Elect please come forward?

[When they have reached the dismissal area, he walks over to them and continues with these words:]

My dear friends,
   on this evening Catholics throughout the world
      remember that our Lord Jesus gave us himself
      under the form of bread and wine,
         for nourishment on our spiritual journey.

Soon you, my dear Elect,
   will be joining us at the Eucharistic banquet.
At that time you will pray the prayer with us
   that Jesus himself entrusted to his disciples.

Since antiquity this prayer has been part of our
   Communion rite—the praying together by the entire
   community of the Our Father.

In the Our Father, we pray: "Thy kingdom come."
   That kingdom is not just something in the future;
      it is involved in the here and now—
      as we minister to one another.

[Presider now blesses the prayer card or missal and hands it to each of the Elect. If the individual has already been baptized in another faith tradition he says:]

(Name of individual/s), you have known this prayer
   through your previous faith tradition.
We ask that you now pray it often during these
   final days of preparation

for the day you will pray it with us
and be nourished by the Eucharist,
the body and blood of the Lord Jesus.

[If the individual has not been baptized, he says:]

(Name of individual/s), we are happy to share
with you
our ancient heritage of faith and prayer.
We ask that you now pray the Our Father
often during these coming days
as you prepare for the day
you will pray it with us
and be nourished by the Eucharist,
the body and blood of the Lord Jesus.

[The presider now touches / embraces each of the Elect and says:]

My dear Elect,
we send you forth from our midst lovingly
so you may ponder
what you have seen,
what you have heard,
and what you have experienced this evening.
Our prayers go with you
as you prepare to join us
at the Eucharistic banquet
during the Easter Vigil.

Prayer of the faithful:

For our Elect, that they may have a living faith in the
Eucharistic presence of Jesus, let us pray to the Lord.

Dismissal based on the presentation of the Our Father.

Good Friday—Presentation of the Creed (A)

[After the veneration of the cross, the presider says:]

Would our Elect please come forward?

[When they have reached the dismissal area, he walks over to them and continues with these words:]

**You, my dear Elect,
have entered into our remembering
of the Lord's passion and death.**

**This memory is part of our profession of faith.
In the Nicene Creed, which we pray each Sunday,
Catholics profess:**

**"For our sake he was crucified,
under Pontius Pilate;
he suffered, died, and was buried."**

[Presider now blesses the prayer card or missal and hands it to each of the Elect. If the individual has already been baptized in another faith tradition he says:]

(Name of individual/s), the Creed has been a part of your religious tradition and has nurtured your faith throughout the years.

**Now, we, your Catholic faith community,
hand it over to you anew,
asking that you once again accept this statement
of belief.**

[If the individual has not been baptized, he says:]

(Name of individual/s), this is the statement of our faith.

It is a precious part of our heritage
which we, as your parish family,
entrust to you
   as you begin your final preparation
   for baptism and full sacramental life
      as a Catholic.

We now ask that you accept it
as your profession of faith.

[The presider now touches/embraces each of the Elect and says:]

We lovingly send you forth from this community
   to ponder what you have heard,
   what you have seen,
   and what you have experienced this evening.

Take with you your Creed.
Our prayers go with you as you prepare
   to join with us at the Eucharistic table
      this Easter Vigil.

Prayer of the faithful:

That our Elect, along with the Elect throughout the
world, may allow the death of the Lord to touch their
personal lives, we pray to the Lord.

Dismissal based on presentation of the Creed.

Easter (A)

(This dismissal is only used if there are candidates and catechumens present. The neophytes remain for the entire liturgy.)

[After the proclamation of the gospel or after the homily, the presider says:]

> **Would our candidates and catechumens please come forward?**

[When they have reached the dismissal area, he walks over to them and dismisses them with these words:]

> **My dear candidates and catechumens,**
>> **let us celebrate the joy of the Risen Lord this Easter.**
>>> **May you dare to trust**
>>>> **that God has affirmed**
>>>> **all that you hope for . . . and much more.**
>
>> **May you live this week joyfully**
>>> **in the embrace of the Risen Lord.**
>
>> **Go now in the peace of Christ**
>>> **to reflect on the Scriptures**
>>> **and break open the Word of God in your lives.**

Prayer of the faithful:

> **For our neophytes, those who were baptized and brought into full communion with our faith community at the Easter Vigil, that they may worship with us in joy, let us pray to the Lord.**
> **For our candidates and catechumens, that they may more deeply trust in the Lord and experience the joy that he alone can give them, let us pray to the Lord.**

Dismissal based on the theme of the feast.

Second Sunday of Easter (A)

[After the proclamation of the gospel or after the homily, the presider says:]

> **Would our candidates and catechumens please come forward?**

[When they have reached the dismissal area, he walks over to them and dismisses them with these words:]

> **My dear candidates and catechumens,**
>> **as we celebrate the joy of the Risen Lord this Eastertide,**
>> **may you experience the peace of the Risen Christ, his gift to each of you.**
>
> **This community now sends you forth**
>> **to reflect more deeply on the Word of God which you have shared with us this morning.**
>
> **Be assured of our loving support and prayers for you.**
>> **We look forward to the day when you will share fully with us at the Eucharistic table.**

Prayer of the faithful:

> **For our neophytes, those brought into full communion with us at the Easter Vigil, that they may experience being one heart and one mind with this community of believers, let us pray to the Lord.**
> **For our candidates and catechumens, that they may grow in faith and make Thomas' words their own: "My Lord and my God," we pray to the Lord.**

Dismissal based on John 20:19-31.

46

Third Sunday of Easter (A)

[After the proclamation of the gospel or after the homily, the presider says:]

> **Would our candidates and catechumens please come forward?**

[When they have reached the dismissal area, he walks over to them and dismisses them with these words:]

> **My dear candidates and catechumens,**
> > **the Lord Jesus, risen from the grave,**
> > > **walked with his disciples along the way.**
> > **We ask this same Lord,**
> > > **to walk now with you, our candidates and catechumens.**
> > **May his words also cause your hearts**
> > > **to burn with love and joy**
> > > **as you reflect on the meaning**
> > > > **of the Scriptures proclaimed in our midst.**
>
> > **Go now in the peace of Christ**
> > > **and be nourished by the Word of God.**
> > > **We look forward to the day when you will also**
> > > **be nourished at the Eucharistic table.**

Prayer of the faithful:

> **For our neophytes, those brought into full communion with us at the Easter Vigil, that they may continue to know Jesus in the "breaking of the bread," let us pray to the Lord.**
> **For our candidates and catechumens, that their minds and hearts may be open to the Scriptures as they are nourished on the Word of God, let us pray to the Lord.**

Dismissal based on Luke 24:13-35.

Fourth Sunday of Easter (A)

[After the proclamation of the gospel or after the homily, the presider says:]

> **Would our candidates and catechumens please come forward?**

[When they have reached the dismissal area, he walks over to them and dismisses them with these words:]

> **My dear candidates and catechumens,**
>   **the Lord Jesus is our Good Shepherd**
>   **who helps those who place their trust in him.**
>   **May each of you recognize his voice**
>   **so that you may live in the confidence**
>   **of his daily care for you,**
>   **and may follow him**
>   **to the fullness of eternal life.**
>
> **Go now in the peace of Christ**
>   **and be nourished on the Word of God.**
> **Be assured of our loving support and prayers**
>   **for you**
>   **as we look forward to the day**
>   **when you will also join us to be nourished**
>   **at the Eucharistic table.**

Prayer of the faithful:

> **For our neophytes, those brought into full communion with us at the Easter Vigil, that they may continue to experience the power of the Risen Lord working in their lives, let us pray to the Lord.**
> **For our candidates and catechumens, that they may believe in God's great love for them as they break open the Word of the Lord and reflect on its meaning in their lives, let us pray to the Lord.**

Dismissal based on John 10:1-10.

Fifth Sunday of Easter (A)

[After the proclamation of the gospel or after the homily, the presider says:]

> **Would our candidates and catechumens please come forward?**

[When they have reached the dismissal area, he walks over to them and dismisses them with these words:]

> **My dear candidates and catechumens,**
> > **the Lord Jesus, our Risen Savior,**
> > > **is the way, the truth and the life**
> > > **for each of us.**
>
> > **May you come to realize**
> > > **the centrality that he wishes to have in your lives**
> > > **and the tenderness with which he loves you.**
>
> > **Go now in the peace of Christ**
> > > **to ponder what you have heard,**
> > > **to take it to heart**
> > > **so that you may be nourished throughout the week.**

Prayer of the faithful:

> **For our neophytes, those brought into full communion with us at the Easter Vigil, that they feel at home in our parish family, let us pray to the Lord.**
> **For our candidates and catechumens, that they may realize that Jesus is the source of true life, let us pray to the Lord.**

Dismissal based on John 14:1-12.

Sixth Sunday of Easter (A)

[After the proclamation of the gospel or after the homily, the presider says:]

> Would our candidates and catechumens please come forward?

[When they have reached the dismissal area, he walks over to them and dismisses them with these words:]

> My dear candidates and catechumens,
>> we ask that the Risen Lord touch each of you
>>> with the joy and peace of this Easter season.
>> As a people of hope,
>>> though not always free from suffering,
>>> may you be surrounded by and filled with love.
>
>> Go now in the peace of Christ
>>> to reflect on the Word of God.
>>> Be assured that you do not travel
>>>> your faith journey alone,
>>>> but as members of this Christian community.
>>> We look forward to the day when you will gather
>>>> with us
>>> to be nourished at the Eucharistic table.

Prayer of the faithful:

> For our neophytes, those brought into full communion with us at the Easter Vigil, that they may experience the love of the Lord in this parish family, let us pray to the Lord.
> For our candidates and catechumens, that they may truly be nourished by the Word of God, proclaimed in our midst today, let us pray to the Lord.

Dismissal based on John 14:15-21.

Seventh Sunday of Easter (A)

[After the proclamation of the gospel or after the homily, the presider says:]

Would our candidates and catechumens please come forward?

[When they have reached the dismissal area, he walks over to them and dismisses them with these words:]

My dear candidates and catechumens,
  may the Risen Christ
    pour out his tenderness and strength on you
    as you continue to ponder his words
      in the Scriptures.

Risen Lord,
  encourage these our candidates and catechumens,
  that they may never lose heart
    as they face the difficulties of life.

Go now in the peace of Christ
  and be assured of our loving support
  and prayers for you.
  We look forward to the day when you will gather
    with us
  to be nourished at the Eucharistic table.

Prayer of the faithful:

For our neophytes, those brought into full communion with us at the Easter Vigil, that they may always have the courage to live their faith, let us pray to the Lord.
For our candidates and catechumens, that they may continue to be open to the Word of God and find nourishment in the Scriptures, let us pray to the Lord.

Dismissal based on John 17:1-11.

Pentecost (A)

[After the proclamation of the gospel or after the homily, the presider says:]

> **Would our candidates and catechumens please come forward?**

[When they have reached the dismissal area, he walks over to them and dismisses them with these words:]

> **My dear candidates and catechumens,**
>> **like the disciples,**
>>> **we are gathered together as a community in prayer.**
>>> **Even closed doors and fearful hearts**
>>>> **do not hinder God's spirit from reaching us.**
>
> **May each of you experience the spirit of the Lord**
>> **working in your lives**
>> **as you reflect on today's Scriptures.**
>
> **Go now in the peace of Christ,**
>> **that peace which he gives each of you,**
>> **and be nourished by the Word of God.**

Prayer of the faithful:

> **For our neophytes, that they may experience the Holy Spirit working in their lives and calling them to ministry, let us pray to the Lord.**
> **That the Holy Spirit may continue to guide our candidates and catechumens and fill their hearts with his love, let us pray to the Lord.**

Dismissal based on the theme of the feast.

Trinity Sunday (A)

[After the proclamation of the gospel or after the homily, the presider says:]

Would our candidates and catechumens please come forward?

[When they have reached the dismissal area, he walks over to them and dismisses them with these words:]

My dear candidates and catechumens,
in our celebration of Trinity Sunday today,
we pray that God the Father, God the Son,
and God the Holy Spirit be revealed to you.

May the God of tenderness, the God of compassion,
and the God of love and faithfulness
touch each of your lives.

May you always be open to the mystery
of the presence and love of the Triune God,
as you continue your journey of faith
into full communion with this community.

Go now in the peace of Christ,
and be nourished with the Word of God.
We look forward to the day when you will gather
with us
to be nourished at the Eucharistic table.

Prayer of the faithful:

For our candidates and catechumens, that they may be
ever open to the mystery of the presence and love of
the Triune God in their lives, let us pray to the Lord.

Dismissal based on the theme of the feast.

The Body and Blood of Christ (A)

[After the proclamation of the gospel or after the homily, the presider says:]

> **Would our candidates and catechumens please come forward?**

[When they have reached the dismissal area, he walks over to them and dismisses them with these words:]

> **My dear candidates and catechumens,**
> **today we celebrate the reality**
> **that the Lord Jesus gave himself to us**
> **under the form of bread and wine.**
>
> **May each of you grow in a realization of the**
> **real presence**
> **of the Lord in the Eucharist,**
> **and come to a better understanding**
> **that in the Eucharist**
> **we are united to the Lord Jesus**
> **and to one another.**
>
> **Go now in the peace of Christ**
> **and be nourished with the Word of God.**
> **We look forward to the day when you will gather**
> **with us**
> **to be nourished by Jesus himself in the Eucharist.**

Prayer of the faithful:

> **That our candidates and catechumens may grow in an appreciation for the sacrament of the Eucharist, let us pray to the Lord.**

Dismissal based on John 6:51-58.

Second Sunday of Ordinary Time (A)

[After the proclamation of the gospel or after the homily, the presider says:]

Would our candidates and catechumens please come forward?

[When they have reached the dismissal area, he walks over to them and dismisses them with these words:]

My dear candidates and catechumens,
Paul's words to the Corinthians are addressed
to each of us this morning.
We are called to be a "holy people."
We are called to wholeness:
to union with God and one another.

May each of you grow in an understanding
of your call to holiness.
and what this call means in your daily life.

Go now in the peace of Christ
to reflect on the Scriptures
and break open the Word of God in your lives.

Prayer of the faithful:

That our candidates and catechumens may grow in an understanding of their call to holiness and what this call means in their daily lives, let us pray to the Lord.

Dismissal based on 1 Cor 1:1-3.

Third Sunday of Ordinary Time (A)

[After the proclamation of the gospel or after the homily, the presider says:]

> **Would our candidates and catechumens please come forward?**

[When they have reached the dismissal area, he walks over to them and dismisses them with these words:]

> **My dear candidates and catechumens,**
>> **"The kingdom of God is at hand."**
>>> **It is in the present, in the here and now,**
>>> **but it is up to each of us**
>>>> **to make its presence known.**
>>> **That is our mission and that is your mission.**
>
>> **May the challenge of today's Word of God**
>>> **echo in your hearts throughout the week.**
>>> **And may your efforts make the kingdom of God**
>>>> **more of a reality for all those**
>>>> **whose lives you touch.**
>
>> **Go now in the peace of Christ to find nourishment**
>>> **in the Word of God.**

Prayer of the faithful:

> **That our candidates and catechumens may help to bring the kingdom to reality in their own lives, let us pray to the Lord.**

Dismissal based on Matt 4:12-23.

Fourth Sunday of Ordinary Time (A)

[After the proclamation of the gospel or after the homily, the presider says:]

Would our candidates and catechumens please come forward?

[When they have reached the dismissal area, he walks over to them and dismisses them with these words:]

My dear candidates and catechumens,
   today the beatitudes have again been proclaimed.
May you come to understand the meaning
   of the attitudes and values expressed in them.
For Jesus tells us that we will be happy
   if we learn to incorporate these values and
      attitudes
   into our daily lives.

Go now and be nourished on the Scriptures
   and break open the Word of God in your lives.

Prayer of the faithful:

For our candidates and catechumens, that they, along with the entire community gathered here, may come to understand the meaning of the values expressed in the beatitudes and incorporate these values and attitudes into daily living, let us pray to the Lord.

Dismissal based on Matt 5:1-12.

Fifth Sunday of Ordinary Time (A)

[After the proclamation of the gospel or after the homily, the presider says:]

Would our candidates and catechumens please come forward?

[When they have reached the dismissal area, he walks over to them and dismisses them with these words:]

My dear candidates and catechumens,
in today's readings we are confronted with the fact
that if we wish to follow Jesus we cannot ignore
the challenge to shelter and to share.
Only in *living* as a follower of Jesus
will our own experience of darkness and gloom,
our own depressions be lifted.

May you give serious consideration to what Jesus
is saying to you when he tells you that
you are the light of the world
and that your light must shine,
so that others may see goodness
in your actions and give praise
to your heavenly Father.

Go now in the peace of Christ to be nourished
by his Word.

Prayer of the faithful:

For our candidates and catechumens, that the Lord may fill their hearts with his brightness and light, so they may enrich the lives of all they meet this week, let us pray to the Lord.

Dismissal based on Isa 58:7-10; Matt 5:13-16.

Sixth Sunday of Ordinary Time (A)

[After the proclamation of the gospel or after the homily, the presider says:]

Would our candidates and catechumens please come forward?

[When they have reached the dismissal area, he walks over to them and dismisses them with these words:]

My dear candidates and catechumens,
**   the Lord calls each of us to be at peace**
**   with one another.**
**   He calls us to a spiritual maturity**
**   which involves a forgiving heart.**
Through the *power of his Word,* may each of you
**   overcome any indifference, any anger,**
**   you may have for those who have been**
**   stumbling blocks in your lives.**

Go now in the peace of Christ to be nourished
**   on the Word of God.**
We look forward to the day when you will also
**   gather with us**
**   around the Eucharistic table.**

Prayer of the faithful:

That our candidates and catechumens may take
seriously the challenge to grow in spiritual maturity,
let us pray to the Lord.

Dismissal based on 1 Cor 2:6-10; Matt 5:17-37.

Seventh Sunday of Ordinary Time (A)

[After the proclamation of the gospel or after the homily, the presider says:]

Would our candidates and catechumens please come forward?

[When they have reached the dismissal area, he walks over to them and dismisses them with these words:]

**My dear candidates and catechumens,
we have heard the call to holiness
in all of the Scripture readings today.**

**And now each of us must ask ourselves:
"How am I responding to that call?"
"What needs to be reformed in me
so that I become more of the beautiful, whole
person that God is calling me to be?"**

**May each of you accept the challenge of today's
Scriptures,
and be open to the ways God is calling you to grow.
May you support one another in your efforts
to truly belong to Christ.
Go now in the peace of Christ to be nourished
by his Word.**

Prayer of the faithful:

**That our candidates and catechumens may be open to
the ways the Lord is calling them to grow in love and
holiness, let us pray to the Lord.**

For this community gathered here in worship, that we may be willing to manifest our love for one another, and particularly for our candidates and catechumens who have come to us in their journey to Christ, let us pray to the Lord.

Dismissal based on Lev 19:1-2, 17-18; 1 Cor 3:16-23; Matt 5:38-48.

Eighth Sunday of Ordinary Time (A)

[After the proclamation of the gospel or after the homily, the presider says:]

Would our candidates and catechumens please come forward?

[When they have reached the dismissal area, he walks over to them and dismisses them with these words:]

My dear candidates and catechumens,
   it is part of being human
      to experience worry and anxiety,
      to want to be in control of the various aspects
         of our lives.
   But it is part of being Christian
      to do what we can, and then
      to place those worries and concerns
         in the hands of God.

May you be assured that the Lord loves and cares
      for you.
   And then you can be even more assured
      that he is present
      even in the difficult concerns of life.

Go now in the peace of Christ to ponder
      the Scriptures
   and be nourished by them.
   This week, may you rely more on God
      than on yourselves.

Prayer of the faithful:

That our candidates and catechumens may come to realize the goodness of the God who loves and cares for each of them, let us pray to the Lord.

Dismissal based on Matt 6:24-34.

Ninth Sunday of Ordinary Time (A)

[After the proclamation of the gospel or after the homily, the presider says:]

> **Would our candidates and catechumens please come forward?**

[When they have reached the dismissal area, he walks over to them and dismisses them with these words:]

> **My dear candidates and catechumens,**
> > **today's Scripture readings have us focus**
> > > **our attention**
> > > **on gaining the kingdom of God.**
> > **The choice seems to be ours, and yet,**
> > > **doing the will of God is sometimes not all that clear.**
>
> **It is often that *in prayer***
> > **we are able to see our way more clearly,**
> > **and have the courage to lead lives that indicate**
> > **that we are serious about the kingdom.**
>
> **May your reflections on the Word of God**
> > **encourage you to live as one seeking the kingdom.**
>
> **Go now in the peace of Christ**
> > **to be nourished on the Scriptures.**
> > **We look forward to the day when you will gather with us**
> > **to be nourished at the Eucharistic banquet.**

Prayer of the faithful:

> **For our candidates and catechumens, that they may have the courage to lead lives that indicate their desire to be part of the kingdom of God, let us pray to the Lord.**

Dismissal based on Deut 11:18, 26-28; Matt 7:21-27.

Tenth Sunday of Ordinary Time (A)

[After the proclamation of the gospel or after the homily, the presider says:]

Would our candidates and catechumens please come forward?

[When they have reached the dismissal area, he walks over to them and dismisses them with these words:]

**My dear candidates and catechumens,
the Word of God proclaimed in our midst this
morning
presents us with two people
who answered the Lord's call,
even though they did not know
where it would lead them.**

**God's call has not been stifled.
He still says to each of us: "Follow me."**

**May you learn to listen for God's call
and have the courage to respond wholeheartedly.**

**Go now in the peace of Christ
to ponder what you have heard
and to break open the Word of God in your lives.**

Prayer of the faithful:

**That our candidates and catechumens may be attentive
to the Lord's call to follow him and have the courage
to respond wholeheartedly, let us pray to the Lord.**

Dismissal based on Rom 4:18-25; Matt 9:9-13.

Eleventh Sunday of Ordinary Time (A)

[After the proclamation of the gospel or after the homily, the presider says:]

Would our candidates and catechumens please come forward?

[When they have reached the dismissal area, he walks over to them and dismisses them with these words:]

My dear candidates and catechumens,
would that each of us could realize
that God's kindness and compassionate love
reach out to touch us.

May you take this truth to heart,
looking into your own lives to discover
when you have experienced God's loving care.
Then may you have the courage to extend that same
kindness and compassion to others.
For, as the Scriptures indicate to us today,
the gift received is to be the gift given.

Go now in the peace of Christ
to ponder these Scriptures and bring them to life
in your own lives.
We long for the day when you will gather with us
at the Eucharistic table.

Prayer of the faithful:

That our candidates and catechumens may discover the
kindness and compassionate love of God active in
their own lives, let us pray to the Lord.

Dismissal based on Exod 19:2-6; Matt 9:36–10:8.

Twelfth Sunday of Ordinary Time (A)

[After the proclamation of the gospel or after the homily, the presider says:]

> **Would our candidates and catechumens please come forward?**

[When they have reached the dismissal area, he walks over to them and dismisses them with these words:]

> **My dear candidates and catechumens,**
> > **today's gospel is filled with encouragement**
> > **for each of us.**
> **May you overcome any intimidation or fear**
> > **as you seek to follow Jesus.**
>
> **Know that he is there to support you,**
> > **and gives you this parish family**
> > **so you do not walk your journey alone.**
>
> **May the Scriptures continue**
> > **to be a source of nourishment for you.**
>
> **Go now in the peace of Christ**
> > **to reflect on the Word of God**
> > **and to be encouraged in your faith journey.**
> > **We long for the day when your journey will bring**
> > **you**
> > **to the Eucharistic table.**

Prayer of the faithful:

> **That our candidates and catechumens may find in each of us a source of encouragement as they continue their faith journey into our Catholic faith, let us pray to the Lord.**

Dismissal based on Matt 10:26-33.

Thirteenth Sunday of Ordinary Time (A)

[After the proclamation of the gospel or after the homily, the presider says:]

Would our candidates and catechumens please come forward?

[When they have reached the dismissal area, he walks over to them and dismisses them with these words:]

My dear candidates and catechumens,
Matthew's Gospel today is a challenge.
Jesus asks each of us to take up our cross,
whatever that cross is for us.
But he also lets us know
that we will be coming after him.
He has gone before us in bearing the cross.

You, my dear friends, were signed with his cross
during your rite of welcome.
We pray that you experience Jesus' presence
in the crosses of daily living.

Go now in the peace of Christ
and be nourished by the Word of God.
Be assured of our loving support and prayers
for you
as we look forward to the day
when you will join us at the Eucharistic table.

Prayer of the faithful:

That our candidates and catechumens may experience
Jesus' presence in any crosses they may bear, let us
pray to the Lord.

Dismissal based on Matt 10:37-42.

Fourteenth Sunday of Ordinary Time (A)

[After the proclamation of the gospel or after the homily, the presider says:]

Would our candidates and catechumens please come forward?

[When they have reached the dismissal area, he walks over to them and dismisses them with these words:]

My dear candidates and catechumens,
Jesus tells us today that we should bring
the burdens of life to him and we will be
refreshed.
As you gather together this morning
to reflect on these Scriptures in your lives,
may you entrust any burden in your lives to him.

Jesus reveals to us that his Father is a God
of tenderness and compassion.
When you are weary, turn to the Lord, your God.

Go now in the peace of Christ
to ponder the Scriptures
and break open the Word of God in your lives.
We look forward to the day when you will join us
to be nourished at the Eucharistic table.

Prayer of the faithful:

That our candidates and catechumens may turn to the Lord with their burdens and cares and experience his life-giving concern for each of them, let us pray to the Lord.

Dismissal based on Matt 11:25-30.

Fifteenth Sunday of Ordinary Time (A)

[After the proclamation of the gospel or after the homily, the presider says:]

> **Would our candidates and catechumens please come forward?**

[When they have reached the dismissal area, he walks over to them and dismisses them with these words:]

> **My dear candidates and catechumens,**
> > **as we reflect on how we, as a parish family,**
> > **accept God's Word,**
> **we ask that you consider the type of soil you are**
> **as you listen to the Word of God.**
>
> **We pray that you take the message of the Scriptures**
> > **into your life—**
> **that it may always be for you a double-edged**
> > **sword:**
> > **affirming God's love for you**
> > **and**
> > **challenging you to conversion.**
>
> **Go now in the peace of Christ**
> > **reflecting on our readings for today.**
> > **We look forward to the day when you will gather**
> > **with us**
> > **at the Eucharistic table.**

Prayer of the faithful:

> **That our candidates and catechumens may be as fertile soil, nourished by the Word of the Lord, let us pray to the Lord.**

Dismissal based on Isa 55:10-11; Matt 13:1-23.

Sixteenth Sunday of Ordinary Time (A)

[After the proclamation of the gospel or after the homily, the presider says:]

Would our candidates and catechumens please come forward?

[When they have reached the dismissal area, he walks over to them and dismisses them with these words:]

My dear candidates and catechumens,
   may you desire to be the field
      where the good seed is sown.

May you learn to recognize evil, for what it is,
   and stand strong in your belief that God is good,
   and that he continues to draw goodness
      from each of you.

Go now in the peace of Christ
   to be nourished by the Scriptures.
   We look forward to the day when you join with us
      at the Eucharistic table.

Prayer of the faithful:

That our candidates and catechumens may be strengthened in their belief that God desires to draw goodness from each of them, let us pray to the Lord.

Dismissal based on Matt 13:24-43.

Seventeenth Sunday of Ordinary Time (A)

[After the proclamation of the gospel or after the homily, the presider says:]

Would our candidates and catechumens please come forward?

[When they have reached the dismissal area, he walks over to them and dismisses them with these words:]

**My dear candidates and catechumens,
the kingdom of heaven is compared
to a treasure in a field.
It is hidden in the Word of God,
which you seek to discover each Sunday.
It is hidden under the sign of bread
in the Eucharist.
It is hidden here in our parish family,
gathered together in worship.
May you be blessed + + + as you look for this
treasure.**

[Here bless each candidate and catechumen and continue:]

**We pray that you may discover this treasure
in your reflections on the Scriptures,
and we long for you to eventually discover it
at the Eucharistic table with us.
Go now in the peace of Christ
and be nourished by the Word of God.**

Prayer of the faithful:

**That our candidates and catechumens may experience
the treasures God holds out to them at this stage in
their faith journey, let us pray to the Lord.**

Dismissal based on Matt 13:44-52.

Eighteenth Sunday of Ordinary Time (A)

[After the proclamation of the gospel or after the homily, the presider says:]

> **Would our candidates and catechumens please come forward?**

[When they have reached the dismissal area, he walks over to them and dismisses them with these words:]

> **My dear candidates and catechumens,**
>> **you have listened to the words of Scripture**
>>> **as proclaimed here in your parish family.**
>
> **May you take these words to heart**
>> **and grow in your realization**
>>> **that nothing can separate you from the love of God**
>>>> **that comes to you in Christ Jesus, our Lord.**
>
> **I bless you now ✝ ✝ ✝ as you go forth to ponder**
>> **the meaning of the Scriptures in your lives.**
> **We eagerly await the day**
>> **when you will share with us**
>>> **at the Eucharistic table.**

Prayer of the faithful:

> **That a deep conviction of Jesus' great love may fill the hearts of our candidates and catechumens and encourage them as they continue their faith journey into our community, let us pray to the Lord.**

Dismissal based on Rom 8:35, 37-39.

Nineteenth Sunday of Ordinary Time (A)

[After the proclamation of the gospel or after the homily, the presider says:]

> **Would our candidates and catechumens please come forward?**

[When they have reached the dismissal area, he walks over to them and dismisses them with these words:]

> **My dear candidates and catechumens,**
> **Matthew's Gospel presents us with a familiar scene.**
> **All of us have experienced the boats of our lives**
> **shaken by the winds and waves.**
>
> **May each of you learn to see**
> **that during the storms, winds, and waves,**
> **the many forms his outstretched hand may take**
> **as Jesus continues to reach out to you.**
>
> **Go now in the peace of Christ**
> **to reflect on the Scriptures**
> **and break open the Word of God in your lives.**

Prayer of the faithful:

> **That our candidates and catechumens may recognize**
> **God's grace in both the positive and negative events of**
> **their lives, let us pray to the Lord.**

Dismissal based on Matt 14:22-33.

Twentieth Sunday of Ordinary Time (A)

[After the proclamation of the gospel or after the homily, the presider says:]

> **Would our candidates and catechumens please come forward?**

[When they have reached the dismissal area, he walks over to them and dismisses them with these words:]

> **My dear candidates and catechumens,**
>   **we have listened to the Scriptures**
>   **proclaimed in our midst.**
>   **Let us pray that each of us may, like Jesus,**
>   **overcome the prejudices of our culture.**
>   **May we learn to respond to the people**
>   **who need us the most.**
>
> **Reflect, then, my friends,**
>   **on the challenge that is ours:**
>   **to love and serve the Lord,**
>   **even when it is difficult to recognize him.**
>
> **Go now in the peace of Christ**
>   **to be nourished on the Word of God.**
>   **We look forward to that day when you will join us**
>   **as we gather together at the Eucharistic table.**

Prayer of the faithful:

> **That our candidates and catechumens will come to realize that they are members of a universal Church into which all nations are welcome, let us pray to the Lord.**

Dismissal based on Matt 15:21-28.

Twenty-First Sunday of Ordinary Time (A)

[After the proclamation of the gospel or after the homily, the presider says:]

> **Would our candidates and catechumens please come forward?**

[When they have reached the dismissal area, he walks over to them and dismisses them with these words:]

> **My dear candidates and catechumens,**
> **you have heard the Scriptures proclaimed this**
> **morning.**
> **May you grow in an understanding**
> **that Jesus gave his disciples the power**
> **to bind and to loose.**
>
> **The sacrament of reconciliation,**
> **is for this community,**
> **an expression of that power,**
> **an experience whereby we too come to**
> **experience**
> **who Jesus is—a God of mercy**
> **and compassionate love.**
>
> **Go now in the peace of Christ**
> **to reflect on the Scriptures**
> **and break open the Word of God in your lives.**

Prayer of the faithful:

> **That our candidates and catechumens may come to**
> **trust and love Holy Mother Church as she continues**
> **her effort to welcome and nourish them, let us pray to**
> **the Lord.**

For those who minister to our candidates and catechumens, that they may continue to manifest the Church's loving care to these new members of our faith community, let us pray to the Lord.

Dismissal based on Matt 16:13-20.

Twenty-Second Sunday of Ordinary Time (A)

[After the proclamation of the gospel or after the homily, the presider says:]

Would our candidates and catechumens please come forward?

[When they have reached the dismissal area, he walks over to them and dismisses them with these words:]

My dear candidates and catechumens,
  may the Lord Jesus, who loves each of you
    impart to you the faith,
    grace you with the courage,
      to really believe his promise:
    that to lose your life for his sake,
      means finding it—
        a more abundant life that abides—
        that cannot be destroyed by death or sin.

Go now in the peace of Christ
  to reflect on the Scriptures
  and break open the Word of God in your lives.

Prayer of the faithful:

That our candidates and catechumens may have the courage and faith to really believe that to lose one's life for Jesus' sake means finding a more abundant life that cannot be destroyed by sin or death, let us pray to the Lord.

Dismissal based on Matt 16:21-27.

Twenty-Third Sunday of Ordinary Time (A)

[After the proclamation of the gospel or after the homily, the presider says:]

> **Would our candidates and catechumens please come forward?**

[When they have reached the dismissal area, he walks over to them and dismisses them with these words:]

> **My dear candidates and catechumens,**
> > **we have all just heard a real challenge—**
> > > **to love our neighbor as we love ourselves.**
>
> **As you gather together this morning,**
> > **reflect on how God is calling you to let his Word**
> > **find meaning in your lives.**
> **May you realize God's abiding love for you**
> > **and may that realization free you**
> > **to forgive all those who have ever hurt you.**
>
> **Go now in the peace of Christ**
> > **to ponder the Scriptures**
> > **and break open the Word of God in your lives.**

Prayer of the faithful:

> **That our candidates and catechumens may experience God's abiding love for them, and that the realization of his love may free them to forgive anyone who may be in need of their forgiveness, let us pray to the Lord.**

Dismissal based on Matt 18:15-20.

Twenty-Fourth Sunday of Ordinary Time (A)

[After the proclamation of the gospel or after the homily, the presider says:]

Would our candidates and catechumens please come forward?

[When they have reached the dismissal area, he walks over to them and dismisses them with these words:]

My dear candidates and catechumens,
 once again the message from the Scriptures
  reminds us
 of the forgiveness we are to offer to one another.
As the Lord is kind and merciful,
 so may you be to all those who touch your lives.
 We are called to forgive without limit,
 and, in so doing,
 we become a reflection of Christ's eternal love.

Go now in the peace of Christ
 to ponder the Scriptures
 and break open the Word of God in your lives.

Prayer of the faithful:

That we, along with our candidates and catechumens, may have the freedom to offer forgiveness to all who are in need of our forgiving love, let us pray to the Lord.

Dismissal based on Matt 18:21-35.

Twenty-Fifth Sunday of Ordinary Time (A)

[After the proclamation of the gospel or after the homily, the presider says:]

> Would our candidates and catechumens please come forward?

[When they have reached the dismissal area, he walks over to them and dismisses them with these words:]

> My dear candidates and catechumens,
>> God cannot be outdone in generosity!
>>> And so we need not be surprised by the parable
>>> just proclaimed in the gospel.
>> But in our listening,
>>> did we discern God as the generous Master
>>> and ourselves as the workers who have come late
>>> in the afternoon?
>> May you take this understanding of the parable to
>>> heart:
>>> looking into your own lives to discover
>>>> when you have experienced God's generosity.
>>> Then may you have the courage to extend
>>>> that same generosity to others.
>
> Go now in the peace of Christ
>> to ponder the Scriptures
>> and bring them to life in your own lives.

Prayer of the faithful:

> That we, along with our candidates and catechumens,
> may activate the challenge of today's parable and
> allow our generosity to go beyond the limits of justice,
> let us pray to the Lord.

Dismissal based on Matt 20:1-16.

Twenty-Sixth Sunday of Ordinary Time (A)

[After the proclamation of the gospel or after the homily, the presider says:]

Would our candidates and catechumens please come forward?

[When they have reached the dismissal area, he walks over to them and dismisses them with these words:]

My dear candidates and catechumens,
this morning Christ Jesus is presented as our model
and we are called to be united in spirit and ideals,
not acting out of rivalry or conceit.
Rather, we are called to make our attitude
the same as Christ's.

May each of you grow in spiritual maturity,
unselfishly and humbly looking to others' needs
rather than your own.

Go now in the peace of Christ
to ponder the Scriptures
and break open the Word of God in your lives.

Prayer of the faithful:

That we, along with our candidates and catechumens, may continue to grow in spiritual maturity, let us pray to the Lord.

Dismissal based on Phil 2:1-11.

Twenty-Seventh Sunday of Ordinary Time (A)

[After the proclamation of the gospel or after the homily, the presider says:]

> **Would our candidates and catechumens please come forward?**

[When they have reached the dismissal area, he walks over to them and dismisses them with these words:]

> **My dear candidates and catechumens,**
>> **may you indeed dismiss all anxieties from your minds**
>>> **and entrust your needs to God**
>>> **in grateful prayer.**
>> **Then you will experience God's own peace**
>>> **which is beyond our comprehension**
>>> **but gives us great peace**
>>> **and the strength to embrace God's will.**
>
> **That is not an easy task**
>> **but it is a necessary step along our faith journey.**
>
> **Go now in the peace of Christ**
>> **to reflect on the meaning of the Scriptures**
>>> **in your lives.**
>
> **Find nourishment in the Scriptures**
>> **as they prepare you to join with us**
>> **at the Eucharistic table.**

Prayer of the faithful:

> **That our candidates and catechumens may entrust their anxieties and concerns to the Lord, knowing that he will care for them, let us pray to the Lord.**

Dismissal based on Phil 4:6-9.

Twenty-Eighth Sunday of Ordinary Time (A)

[After the proclamation of the gospel or after the homily, the presider says:]

> Would our candidates and catechumens please come forward?

[When they have reached the dismissal area, he walks over to them and dismisses them with these words:]

> My dear candidates and catechumens,
> each of you has been invited to the banquet of life!
> May you grow in an awareness of this gracious
> invitation
> and respond wholeheartedly
> as you continue your faith journey with us.
>
> Jesus invites you to the banquet of his Word
> and it is he alone who can satisfy your
> deepest needs
> and make you whole by his love.
>
> Go now in the peace of Christ
> to be nourished with the Word of God.
> We look forward to the day when you will gather
> with us
> to be nourished with the Bread of Life.

Prayer of the faithful:

> That our candidates and catechumens may grow in
> their awareness that the Lord alone can satisfy their
> deepest needs and make them whole by his love, let
> us pray to the Lord.

Dismissal based on Isa 25:6-10; Matt 22:1-14.

Twenty-Ninth Sunday of Ordinary Time (A)

[After the proclamation of the gospel or after the homily, the presider says:]

> Would our candidates and catechumens please come forward?

[When they have reached the dismissal area, he walks over to them and dismisses them with these words:]

> My dear candidates and catechumens,
> as you gather this morning to reflect on today's
>   Scriptures,
>   may you be increasingly aware
>   that earthly concerns cannot be allowed
>   to cloud over your response
>   to God's invitation to his kingdom.
>
> Each day this week,
> may your faith, your hope, and your love
> be revealed in your everyday lives.
> This will be the way that you make the kingdom
>   of God
> present to all those you meet.
>
> Go now in the peace of Christ
> to ponder the Scriptures
> and break open the Word of God in your lives.

Prayer of the faithful:

> That we, along with our candidates and catechumens, may increasingly realize that our faith is real only if it influences our lives each day, let us pray to the Lord.

Dismissal based on Matt 22:15-21.

Thirtieth Sunday of Ordinary Time (A)

[After the proclamation of the gospel or after the homily, the presider says:]

> **Would our candidates and catechumens please come forward?**

[When they have reached the dismissal area, he walks over to them and dismisses them with these words:]

> **My dear candidates and catechumens,**
> **the Word of God proclaimed in our midst**
> **this morning**
> **offers each of us a challenge to love.**
> **As you reflect on the Scriptures**
> **consider anew**
> **what God is asking from you**
> **at this point in your faith journey.**
> **We pray that you may have the courage**
> **to accept the challenge of the Scriptures**
> **in your daily lives.**
>
> **Go now in the peace of Christ**
> **and be nourished by the Word of God.**
> **We look forward to the day when you will gather**
> **with us**
> **at the Eucharistic table.**

Prayer of the faithful:

> **That we, along with our candidates and catechumens,**
> **may truly realize Jesus' command that our daily lives**
> **be based on love, let us pray to the Lord.**

Dismissal based on Exod 22:20-26; Matt 22:34-40.

Thirty-First Sunday of Ordinary Time (A)

[After the proclamation of the gospel or after the homily, the presider says:]

> **Would our candidates and catechumens please come forward?**

[When they have reached the dismissal area, he walks over to them and dismisses them with these words:]

> **My dear candidates and catechumens,**
> > **today's gospel indicates that the leaders of Jesus' day**
> > > **were a disappointment to their community.**
> > > **And we know that sometimes our leaders today**
> > > **are a disappointment to us.**
>
> > **As you become more involved in this community**
> > > **remember that the key to leadership**
> > > > **is to put your gifts and talents**
> > > > **in the service of others.**
>
> > **Go now in the peace of Christ**
> > > **to ponder the Scriptures**
> > > **and break open the Word of God in your lives.**
> > **We look forward to the day when you will**
> > > **gather with us**
> > > **to be nourished at the Eucharistic meal.**

Prayer of the faithful:

> **That we, along with our candidates and catechumens, may take Jesus' Word to heart and truly offer ourselves in service to one another, let us pray to the Lord.**
> **For those who minister to our candidates and catechumens, that they may continue to manifest the Church's loving care to these new members of our community, let us pray to the Lord.**

Dismissal based on Matt 23:1-12.

Thirty-Second Sunday of Ordinary Time (A)

[After the proclamation of the gospel or after the homily, the presider says:]

Would our candidates and catechumens please come forward?

[When they have reached the dismissal area, he walks over to them and dismisses them with these words:]

My dear candidates and catechumens,
may you grow in wisdom
through your reflections on the Word of God
so that you will truly see
what is right and good;
so that you will keep your goals in mind
and order your actions accordingly.
Like the torch in today's gospel
may your faith be kept alive
and be a source of light to others.

Go now in the peace of Christ
to ponder the Scriptures
and break open the Word of God in your lives.

Prayer of the faithful:

That our candidates and catechumens, along with all the members of this community, grow in the realization that the gift of faith, like the torch in today's gospel, needs to be kept alive, nourished and growing—it cannot be taken for granted, let us pray to the Lord.

Dismissal based on Wis 6:12-16; Matt 25:1-13.

Thirty-Third Sunday of Ordinary Time (A)

[After the proclamation of the gospel or after the homily, the presider says:]

Would our candidates and catechumens please come forward?

[When they have reached the dismissal area, he walks over to them and dismisses them with these words:]

**My dear candidates and catechumens,
the Word of God proclaimed in our midst
this morning
reminds us that one can either take risks,
choose Jesus and be blessed,
or reject Jesus and stagnate.
There seems to be no safe middle path for us
to walk.**

**Take a look at your own spiritual journeys
and consider how much you have let the
Word of God
influence your spiritual growth.**

**Go now in the peace of Christ
to be nourished by the Word of God.
We look forward to the day when you will gather
with us
to be nourished at the Eucharistic table.**

Prayer of the faithful:

**That our candidates and catechumens, along with all
here present in the worshiping community, may
realize that we are individually responsible for our
spiritual growth, let us pray to the Lord.**

Dismissal based on Matt 25:14-30.

Christ the King (A)

[After the proclamation of the gospel or after the homily, the presider says:]

Would our candidates and catechumens please come forward?

[When they have reached the dismissal area, he walks over to them and dismisses them with these words:]

My dear candidates and catechumens,
  the Scriptures proclaimed in our community
      this morning
    on the feast of Christ the King
    speak strongly to all of us.
They challenge us to examine our relationships
    with those persons God has placed in our lives.
As you reflect on these readings
    pray that each member of your parish family,
    along with yourselves,
      may truly be convinced
      that what we do for others, we do for Christ;
      and what we fail to do for others,
      we fail to do for Christ.

  Go now in the peace of Christ
    to break open the Word of God
    and find nourishment for your lives.

Prayer of the faithful:

That we, along with our candidates and catechumens, may be convinced that what we do to others, Christ takes as done to himself, let us pray to the Lord.

Dismissal based on Matt 25:31-46.

First Sunday of Advent (B)

[After the proclamation of the gospel or after the homily, the presider says:]

Would our candidates and catechumens please come forward?

[When they have reached the dismissal area, he walks over to them and dismisses them with these words:]

My dear candidates and catechumens,
  this morning we begin a new liturgical year
    and the gospel reading for this First Sunday
      of Advent
    urges us to watchfulness.
During this season we do not just look forward
  to commemorate Jesus' birth,
  his entering our history.
  Rather we are challenged to recognize
    his entering our daily lives each day,
      and we acknowledge that he will come again
        at the end of time.
And so the theme of watchfulness recalls
  his continual coming and our need to be alert
    to recognize him.

Go now in the peace of Christ
  to ponder the Word of God
  and its meaning in your life this Advent season.

Prayer of the faithful:

That our candidates and catechumens will learn to recognize the Lord as he enters their lives during this Advent, let us pray to the Lord.

Dismissal based on Matt 13:33-37.

Second Sunday of Advent (B)

[After the proclamation of the gospel or after the homily, the presider says:]

> **Would our candidates and catechumens please come forward?**

[When they have reached the dismissal area, he walks over to them and dismisses them with these words:]

> **My dear candidates and catechumens,**
> **today's Advent gospel challenges each of us**
> **with the prophet's call:**
> **to prepare the way of the Lord,**
> **to make straight his paths**
> **into our heart and into our world.**
>
> **May any complacency give way to conversion**
> **as we humbly acknowledge our failures**
> **and accept one another in Christ.**
>
> **Go now in the peace of Christ**
> **and be nourished by the Scriptures**
> **which have been proclaimed in our midst.**
> **We long for the day when you will join with us**
> **at the Eucharistic table.**

Prayer of the faithful:

> **That during this grace-filled Advent season, each of us, along with our candidates and catechumens, may accept the challenge to prepare a way for the Lord, making straight his path into our hearts and our world, let us pray to the Lord.**

Dismissal based on Mark 1:1-8.

Third Sunday of Advent (B)

[After the proclamation of the gospel or after the homily, the presider says:]

> **Would our candidates and catechumens please come forward?**

[When they have reached the dismissal area, he walks over to them and dismisses them with these words:]

> **My dear candidates and catechumens,**
>   **may the God of glory and splendor**
>   **at whose touch the wilderness blooms**
>   **and broken lives are mended,**
>   **open your eyes to his hidden presence**
>   **and loosen your tongues**
>   **in gentleness, compassion, and gratitude.**
>   **May each of you continue your journey**
>   **with perseverance and patience**
>   **during this Advent time of longing and waiting.**
>
> **Go now in the peace of Christ**
>   **to experience his good news in your lives.**
>   **We eagerly await the day when you will join with us**
>   **at the Eucharistic table.**

Prayer of the faithful:

> **That our candidates and catechumens may experience this Advent as a time or rediscovery of the Lord's hidden presence in their lives, let us pray to the Lord.**

Dismissal based on Isa 61:1-2; 10-11.

Fourth Sunday of Advent (B)

[After the proclamation of the gospel or after the homily, the presider says:]

Would our candidates and catechumens please come forward?

[When they have reached the dismissal area, he walks over to them and dismisses them with these words:]

My dear candidates and catechumens,
    we have just heard that nothing is impossible
        with God.
As you gather to be nourished by the Scriptures
    on this final Sunday of Advent,
    may Mary, the Mother of the Lord Jesus,
        help you to trust God
        in all the events of your life.

Go now in the peace of Christ
    ✛ **in the name of the Father**
    and of the Son
    and of the Holy Spirit. Amen.

Prayer of the faithful:

That our candidates and catechumens may see the Lord's goodness and promise working in their own lives, let us pray to the Lord.

Dismissal based on Luke 1:26-38.

Christmas (B)

[After the proclamation of the gospel or after the homily, the presider says:]

> Would our candidates and catechumens please come forward?

[When they have reached the dismissal area, he walks over to them and dismisses them with these words:]

> My dear candidates and catechumens,
>   in the name of our parish family
>   I wish you the peace and joy of Christmas.
>   Today we celebrate the reality of the Incarnation:
>   Jesus took upon himself our flesh
>   to dwell among us and show us what God is like.
>   In doing this, Jesus also showed us
>   what our lives are to be like.
>
> As you continue to reflect on the Scripture readings
>   may the peace, the love, and the joy
>   that Christ came to give each of us
>   find a home in your hearts.
>
> Go now in the peace of Christ.
>   We look forward to the day when you will join
>   with us
>   to be nourished at the Eucharistic table.

Prayer of the faithful:

> That our candidates and catechumens may experience the great love that God has for each of them in the giving of his Son, let us pray to the Lord.

Dismissal based on theme of the feast.

Holy Family (B)

[After the proclamation of the gospel or after the homily, the presider says:]

> **Would our candidates and catechumens please come forward?**

[When they have reached the dismissal area, he walks over to them and dismisses them with these words:]

> **My dear candidates and catechumens,**
> > **as you gather on this feast of the Holy Family**
> > > **to reflect on the message of the Word of God**
> > > **proclaimed in our midst this morning**
> > > **may each of you**
> > > > **be mindful of the family which has nurtured you.**
>
> > **Forgive any grievances you may harbor**
> > > **against another**
> > > **so that you may experience peace**
> > > > **within yourself and in your family.**
> > **Then the Word of God, rich as it is,**
> > > **will truly dwell in your hearts.**
>
> > **Go now in the peace of Christ**
> > > **to be nourished on the Word of God until that day**
> > > **when you will join with us to be nourished**
> > > **at the Eucharistic table.**

Prayer of the faithful:

> **That our candidates and catechumens experience warmth and welcome from us, their parish family, let us pray to the Lord.**

Dismissal based on Col 3:12-21.

Mother of God (B)

[After the proclamation of the gospel or after the homily, the presider says:]

> Would our candidates and catechumens please come forward?

[When they have reached the dismissal area, he walks over to them and dismisses them with these words:]

> My dear candidates and catechumens,
>> on this feast of Mary, the Mother of God,
>>> we pray that each of you may also experience
>>> the graciousness of our God.
>> Like Mary, may you learn to treasure
>>> those times God makes himself known to you
>>> and reflect upon his presence in your lives.
>
> Go now in the peace of Christ
>> and be nourished by the Scriptures
>> proclaimed in our midst.

Prayer of the faithful:

> That our candidates and catechumens may find in Mary, the Mother of God, a model for their own lives, let us pray to the Lord.

Dismissal based on Num 6:22-27; Luke 2:16-21.

Second Sunday after Christmas (B)

[After the proclamation of the gospel or after the homily, the presider says:]

> **Would our candidates and catechumens please come forward?**

[When they have reached the dismissal area, he walks over to them and dismisses them with these words:]

> **My dear candidates and catechumens,**
> **the Letter to the Ephesians which we have just read**
> **expresses our sentiments this morning:**
> **we thank God for you and pray for you,**
> **that you may know more clearly the Lord Jesus**
> **and the love that he has for you.**
> **May your innermost vision be so clarified**
> **that you see how he is calling each of you**
> **into his own likeness**
> **for that is your glorious heritage!**
>
> **Go now in the peace of Christ**
> **to reflect on the Scripture readings**
> **proclaimed in our midst and on the heritage**
> **which is yours in Christ Jesus, our Lord.**

Prayer of the faithful:

> **That our candidates and catechumens may experience**
> **in this community the wealth of their Catholic heritage**
> **and a sense of the hope that is theirs as they continue**
> **their faith journey, let us pray to the Lord.**

Dismissal based on Eph 1:3-6, 15-18.

Epiphany (B)

[After the proclamation of the gospel or after the homily, the presider says:]

Would our candidates and catechumens please come forward?

[When they have reached the dismissal area, he walks over to them and dismisses them with these words:]

My dear candidates and catechumens,
   today we celebrate Epiphany,
      the manifestation of Christ to all the world.
   Today we recall the journey that each of us makes
      in order to be open and offer our gifts.

May each of you experience Christ
   as the light who leads you out of any darkness,
   the light who accompanies you on your journey.

Go now in the peace of Christ to reflect on the
      readings
   proclaimed in our midst.
   We look forward to the day when your journey
   will bring you to the Eucharistic table.

Prayer of the faithful:

That our candidates and catechumens may find our parish family a light to them on their journey into the fullness of our faith community, let us pray to the Lord.

Dismissal based on Matt 2:1-12.

Baptism of the Lord (B)

[After the proclamation of the gospel or after the homily, the presider says:]

> Would our candidates and catechumens please come forward?

[When they have reached the dismissal area, he walks over to them and dismisses them with these words:]

> My dear candidates and catechumens,
>> today's Scriptures speak to us of one who is servant,
>> one who proclaims the good news of peace,
>> one who is proclaimed as "my beloved Son."
>
> May you experience the challenge of the Word of God
>> to bring some element of peace
>> into your own day-by-day worlds.
>
> Go now in the peace of Christ
>> to be nourished by the Scriptures.
>> Be instruments of good news this week.
>> Then you will know that God's favor
>> rests on you, too.

Prayer of the faithful:

> That our candidates and catechumens may more fully realize that those baptized in Jesus' name are responsible to be messengers of his peace and love in their everyday lives, let us pray to the Lord.

Dismissal based on Isa 42:1-4, 6-7; Mark 1:7-11.

First Sunday of Lent (B)

[At the end of the Rite of Sending, the presider addresses the following words to the candidates and catechumens as their dismissal:]

> **And so, my dear Elect,**
> > **in the name of this parish family, I now send you**
> > (Names of the Elect are inserted here.)
> > **to your cathedral this evening**
> > > **to be joined by other catechumens who are seeking**
> > > **baptism in our faith,**
> > > **and other candidates who are seeking**
> > > > **full communion in the Catholic community.**

[The presider extends his hands over the Elect]

> > **You have been chosen by God**
> > > **and have entered with us into this way of Lent.**
> > **May Christ Jesus himself**
> > > **teach you the value of prayer and fasting**
> > > **in meeting temptation,**
> > > > **especially during this time of Lenten retreat.**
>
> > **Go now in peace. Soon you will join with us**
> > > **to be nourished at the Eucharistic table.**

Prayer of the faithful:

> **That all candidates and catechumens may experience**
> **the universality and love of our Catholic faith tradition**
> **as they meet with the bishop for the Rite of Election.**

Dismissal based on Mark 1:12-15.

Optional Dismissal for First Sunday of Lent (B)
(To be used when the Rite of Sending does not take place.)

[After the proclamation of the gospel or after the homily, the presider says:]

Would our candidates and catechumens please come forward?

[When they have reached the dismissal area, he walks over to them and dismisses them with these words:]

My dear candidates and catechumens,
    this morning we begin our Lenten season together.
With Jesus we are also sent into the desert
    to be liberated from the compulsions of the world
    and to open our hearts to the kingdom of God.

We invite you to join with us
    in prayer,
    in fasting,
    and in almsgiving,
      three aspects of our Lenten tradition
      through which God makes his presence
        known to us.

Go now in the peace of Christ
    to be nourished by the Scriptures
    and to enter into our Lenten traditions.

Prayer of the faithful:

That our candidates and catechumens may enter wholeheartedly into the grace-filled season of Lent and may be liberated from the compulsions of our world so that they may be open to the inspirations of the Spirit, let us pray to the Lord.

Dismissal based on theme of the Lenten season.

Second Sunday of Lent (B)

[After the proclamation of the gospel or after the homily, the presider says:]

Would our Elect please come forward?

[When they have reached the dismissal area, he walks over to them and dismisses them with these words:]

My dear Elect,
the term "Christian" implies that one is *Christ-like*.
May today's Scriptures open your eyes
to see those areas in your life
where you *are* Christ-like.

May you also experience God's loving graciousness
helping you to change, transfigure, heal,
any broken areas of your lives.

Go now in the peace of Christ.
We pray for you during this Lenten retreat
and look forward to the day you will join with us
at the Eucharistic table.

Prayer of the faithful:

That our Elect may experience their lives being
transformed by God's loving graciousness, let us pray
to the Lord.

Dismissal based on Mark 9:2-10.

Optional Dismissal for Second Sunday of Lent (B)
(To be used when there are no Elect.)

[After the proclamation of the gospel or after the homily, the presider says:]

Would our candidates and catechumens please come forward?

[When they have reached the dismissal area, he walks over to them and dismisses them with these words:]

**My dear candidates and catechumens,
  the term "Christian" implies that one is *Christ-like*.
May today's Scriptures open your eyes
    to see those areas in your life
    where you *are* Christ-like.**

**May you also experience God's loving graciousness
    helping you to change, transfigure, heal,
    any broken areas of your lives.
Go now in the peace of Christ.
    We pray for you during this Lenten journey
    and look forward to the day you will join with us
    at the Eucharistic table.**

Prayer of the faithful:

**That our candidates and catechumens may experience
their lives transformed by God's loving graciousness,
let us pray to the Lord.**

Dismissal based on Mark 9:2-10.

Third Sunday of Lent (B)

[The great conversion stories are used for the Scrutinies. These are the readings of cycle A and they are used no matter what the current cycle is. At the end of the First Scrutiny the presider addresses the Elect:]

My dear Elect,
your experience and our experience
has been that of the Samaritan woman.
Now may we seek from Jesus
living water:
a water which will help us see ourselves
for who we really are,
a water which will satisfy our deepest longings.

We send you forth to reflect on your experience
and continue to be nourished by the Word of God.

Go now in the peace of Christ.
We eagerly await the day when you will be
joining us
at the Eucharistic banquet.

Prayer of the faithful:

That our Elect may experience Jesus as the "living
water," refreshing them throughout their faith
journey, let us pray to the Lord.

Dismissal based on John 4:5-42.

Optional Dismissal for Third Sunday of Lent (B)

(To be used when there are no Elect.)

[After the proclamation of the gospel or after the homily, the presider says:]

Would our candidates and catechumens please come forward?

[When they have reached the dismissal area, he walks over to them and dismisses them with these words:]

My dear candidates and catechumens,
  today we have heard Paul preach Christ crucified.
During this Lenten season
  we focus our attention on the cross.
Perhaps we need to be aware
  that the crosses in our own lives
  are not absurdities
  and are not meant to be stumbling blocks.

May you grow in the realization that in accepting
  the cross into your own life
  you can experience the power and wisdom of God.

Go now in the peace of Christ
  to ponder and be nourished by the Word of God
  until that day when you will join with us
  to be nourished at the Eucharistic table.

Prayer of the faithful:

That our candidates and catechumens may accept their own crosses and find in that acceptance an experience of the presence of the Lord, let us pray to the Lord.

Dismissal based on 1 Cor 1:22-25.

Fourth Sunday of Lent (B)

[After the end of the Second Scrutiny, the presider addresses the Elect:]

My dear Elect,
    until we meet again at the next scrutiny,
      go in peace,
      and may he who is the Light of the World
      be with each of you.

We send you forth to reflect on the account
    of the man born blind,
    and how that person is you.
Go now in the peace of Christ.
    May you be nourished by the Word of God
      made present in your lives.
    Your parish family longs to have you join with us
      at the banquet of the Eucharist.

Prayer of the faithful:

For our Elect, that they may truly experience the Lord opening their eyes to a Christian vision of the world, let us pray to the Lord.

Dismissal based on John 9:1-41.

Optional Dismissal for Fourth Sunday of Lent (B)

(To be used when there are no Elect.)

[After the proclamation of the gospel or after the homily, the presider says:]

Would our candidates and catechumens please come forward?

[When they have reached the dismissal area, he walks over to them and dismisses them with these words:]

My dear candidates and catechumens,
 you are indeed God's handiwork.
He has gifted you with faith
 and called you from darkness into light.
May you walk in God's light
 with your actions proclaiming to others
 that you want to share the fullness of his love
 to all.

Go now in the peace of Christ
 to be nourished by the Word of God
 into the fullness of life with Christ.

Prayer of the faithful:

That our candidates and catechumens may deliberately choose to share the fullness of life with Christ and that this choice be the motivation of their actions, let us pray to the Lord.

Dismissal based on Eph 2:4-10.

Fifth Sunday of Lent (B)

[At the end of the Third Scrutiny the presider addresses the Elect:]

My dear friends,
   the Lord Jesus raised Lazarus from the dead
      as a sign that he had come
      to give us life in full measure.
May he rescue you, our Elect,
   from all death-dealing situations
   as you seek life in the sacraments.
By his Holy Spirit,
   may he fill each of you with new life,
   increasing your faith, hope, and love,
   so that you may have life to the fullest
      and thus come to share in his resurrection.

My dear Elect,
   we now send you forth to reflect more deeply
      upon the Word of God
      and the events which we have shared today.

Prayer of the faithful:

For our Elect, that they may learn to trust in the Lord
and his power in the death-dealing situations of their
own lives, let us pray to the Lord.

Dismissal based on John 11:1-45.

Optional Dismissal for Fifth Sunday of Lent (B)
(To be used when there are no Elect.)

[After the proclamation of the gospel or after the homily, the presider says:]

Would our candidates and catechumens please come forward?

[When they have reached the dismissal area, he walks over to them and dismisses them with these words:]

My dear candidates and catechumens,
today's gospel brings us face to face with mystery.
A grain of wheat must die,
be buried in the earth in order to experience
new life.
Each of us, through this Lenten season
has been challenged to die to ourselves
through prayer, fasting, and almsgiving,
so that we may experience new life in Christ.

We need to ask ourselves:
what fruits have become realities:
kindness? compassion? intimacy with Jesus?
It is not too late to follow Jesus,
to join with him as a grain of wheat.

Go now in the peace of Christ
to ponder and be nourished by the Word of God.

Prayer of the faithful:

That our candidates and catechumens may be willing
to die to themselves in order to experience new life in
Christ, let us pray to the Lord.

Dismissal based on John 12:20-33.

Passion/Palm Sunday (B)

[After the proclamation of the gospel or after the homily, the presider says:]

Would our Elect please come forward?

[When they have reached the dismissal area, he walks over to them and dismisses them with these words:]

My dear Elect,
you join with us today to begin
the most solemn week of the year.
Holy Mother Church extends to each of you
the fullness of graces and blessings this holy week.
We see Jesus identify himself with us
through his death on the cross.
With arms outstretched he embraces all of us.

Jesus identifies himself with you.
Now it is up to you to consider
how you have identified yourself with him.

Go now to ponder the Scriptures
and what they mean to your life.
Enter deeply into these holy days
as you prepare to be one
with Jesus in the Eucharist.

Prayer of the faithful:

That our Elect may experience an identification of their lives with Christ, let us pray to the Lord.

Dismissal based on Mark 14:1–15:47.

Optional Dismissal Passion/Palm Sunday (B)
(To be used when there are no Elect.)

[After the proclamation of the gospel or after the homily, the presider says:]

Would our candidates and catechumens please come forward?

[When they have reached the dismissal area, he walks over to them and dismisses them with these words:]

My dear candidates and catechumens,
   Jesus identifies himself with us
      through his death on the cross.
   He willingly faces the greatest of our fears—
      annihilation.
   He has identified himself with us,
      now it is up to each of you
      to ponder
      on how you have identified yourself with him
         throughout your Lenten journey.

Go now in the peace of Christ
   to reflect on the Scriptures
   and break open the Word of God in your lives.

Prayer of the faithful:

That through their Lenten journey, our candidates and catechumens become more Christ-like, let us pray to the Lord.

Dismissal based on theme of the Sunday.

Holy Thursday—Presentation of the Our Father with Dismissal (B)

[After the proclamation of the gospel or after the homily, the presider says:]

Would our Elect please come forward?

[When they have reached the dismissal area, he walks over to them and continues with these words:]

My dear friends,
on this evening Catholics throughout the world
remember that our Lord Jesus gave us himself
under the form of bread and wine,
for our spiritual journey.

Soon you, my dear Elect,
will be joining us at the Eucharistic banquet.
At that time you will pray the prayer with us
that Jesus himself entrusted to his disciples.

Since antiquity this prayer has been part of our
Communion rite—the praying together by the
entire community of the Our Father.

In the Our Father we pray: "Thy kingdom come."
That kingdom is not just something in the future:
it is involved in the here and now—
as we minister to one another.

[Presider now blesses the prayer card or missal and hands it to each of the Elect. If the individual has already been baptized in another faith tradition he says:]

(Name of individual/s), you have known this prayer
through your previous faith tradition.

We ask that you now pray it often during these
final days of preparation
for the day you will pray it with us
and be nourished by the Eucharist,
the body and blood of the Lord Jesus.

[If the individual has not been baptized, he says:]

(Name of individual/s), we are happy to share
with you
our ancient heritage of faith and prayer.
We ask that you now pray the Our Father
often during these coming days
as you prepare for the day
you will pray it with us
and be nourished by the Eucharist,
the body and blood of the Lord Jesus.

[The presider now touches/embraces each of the Elect and says:]

My dear Elect,
we send you forth from our midst lovingly
so you may ponder
what you have seen,
what you have heard,
and what you have experienced this evening.
Our prayers go with you
as you prepare to join us
at the Eucharistic banquet
during the Easter Vigil.

Prayer of the faithful:

For our Elect, that they may have a living faith in the
Eucharistic presence of Jesus, let us pray to the Lord.

Dismissal based on the presentation of the Our Father.

Good Friday—Presentation of the Creed with Dismissal (B)

[After the veneration of the cross, the presider says:]

Would our Elect please come forward?

[When they have reached the dismissal area, he walks over to them and continues with these words:]

You, my dear Elect,
 have entered into our remembering
 of the Lord's passion and death.

This memory is part of our profession of faith.
 In the Nicene Creed, which we pray each Sunday,
  Catholics profess:

 "For our sake he was crucified,
  under Pontius Pilate;
 he suffered, died, and was buried."

[Presider now blesses the prayer card or missal and hands it to each of the Elect. If the individual has already been baptized in another faith tradition he says:]

(Name of individual/s), the Creed has been a part of
 your religious tradition and has nurtured your faith
 throughout the years.

Now, we, your Catholic faith community,
 hand it over to you anew,
 asking that you once again accept this statement
 of belief.

[If the individual has not been baptized, he says:]

(Name of individual/s), this is the statement of our
 faith.

It is a precious part of our heritage
which we, as your parish family,
entrust to you
   as you begin your final preparation
   for baptism and full sacramental life
      as a Catholic.

We now ask that you accept it
as your profession of faith.

[The presider now touches/embraces each of the Elect and says:]

We lovingly send you forth from this community
   to ponder what you have heard,
   what you have seen,
   and what you have experienced this evening.

Take with you your Creed.
   Our prayers go with you as you prepare
   to join with us at the Eucharistic table
   this Easter Vigil.

Prayer of the faithful:

That our Elect, along with the Elect throughout the
world, may allow the death of the Lord to touch their
personal lives, we pray to the Lord.

Dismissal based on the presentation of the Creed.

Easter Sunday (B)

(This dismissal is only used if there are candidates and catechumens present. The neophytes remain for the entire liturgy.)

[After the proclamation of the gospel or after the homily, the presider says:]

> **Would our candidates and catechumens please come forward?**

[When they have reached the dismissal area, he walks over to them and dismisses them with these words:]

> **My dear candidates and catechumens,**
> > **let us celebrate the joy of the Risen Lord this Easter.**
> > > **May you dare to trust**
> > > > **that God has affirmed**
> > > > > **all that you hope for . . . and much more.**
>
> > **May you live this week joyfully**
> > > **in the embrace of the Risen Lord.**
>
> **Go now in the peace of Christ**
> > **to reflect on the Scriptures**
> > **and break open the Word of God in your lives.**

Prayer of the faithful:

> **For our neophytes, those brought into full communion with us at the Easter Vigil, that they may worship with us in joy, let us pray to the Lord.**
> **For our candidates and catechumens, that they may trust in the Lord and experience the joy that he alone can give them, let us pray to the Lord.**

Dismissal based on John 20:1-9.

Second Sunday of Easter (B)

[After the proclamation of the gospel or after the homily, the presider says:]

> Would our candidates and catechumens please come forward?

[When they have reached the dismissal area, he walks over to them and dismisses them with these words:]

> My dear candidates and catechumens,
>> the Scripture readings of the Easter season
>>> fill us with great hope.
>>> Jesus greets us with: "Peace be with you."
>> We who are greeted with peace are also blessed,
>>> for unlike Thomas we have not seen Jesus
>>> but have believed in him.
>> May your belief in the Risen Lord
>>> take such a hold on your life
>>> that all your actions may be done
>>> in the light of the resurrection.
>
>> Go now in the peace of Christ
>>> to be nourished on the Scriptures
>>> and to extend his peace
>>> to all the people in your life.

Prayer of the faithful:

> For our neophytes (those brought into full communion with us at the Easter Vigil) that their worship in fullness with us may be a source of deep peace in their lives, let us pray to the Lord.
> That our candidates and catechumens may be strengthened in their belief in the Risen Lord and may experience his peace in their lives, let us pray to the Lord.

Dismissal based on John 20:19-31.

Third Sunday of Easter (B)

[After the proclamation of the gospel or after the homily, the presider says:]

> Would our candidates and catechumens please come forward?

[When they have reached the dismissal area, he walks over to them and dismisses them with these words:]

> My dear candidates and catechumens,
>> our Scripture readings for today cause us to ponder
>> on the meaning of Easter.
>>> We hear Jesus tell us to touch him.
>> How is it that we touch Jesus today?
>>> Through the intimacy of prayer and meditation,
>>> through the kindness and compassion we show others,
>>> through responding to the inspirations of the
>>>> graces he gives us.
>> May each of you respond to his request to touch him
>>> in the unique way that is yours
>>>> to manifest your trust and love for him.
>
>> Go now in the peace of Christ
>>> to ponder the Scriptures
>>> and to be nourished on them
>>> until that day when you will join with us
>>> to be nourished at the Eucharistic table.

Prayer of the faithful:

> That our candidates and catechumens may grow in an intimacy with Jesus, let us pray to the Lord.
> For our neophytes (those brought into full communion with us at the Easter Vigil) that they may be drawn into intimacy with Jesus in the Eucharist, let us pray to the Lord.

Dismissal based on Luke 24:35-48.

118

Fourth Sunday of Easter (B)

[After the proclamation of the gospel or after the homily, the presider says:]

> **Would our candidates and catechumens please come forward?**

[When they have reached the dismissal area, he walks over to them and dismisses them with these words:]

> **My dear candidates and catechumens,**
> > **today Jesus proclaims to us**
> > > **that he is our Good Shepherd,**
> > > **one who is deeply concerned about each of us.**
> > **As you continue your faith journey**
> > > **may you come to know and trust Jesus**
> > > > **and continue to personally experience**
> > > > **his love and concern for you.**
>
> **Go now in the peace of Christ**
> > **and be nourished by the Scriptures.**
> > **We pray that you follow Jesus, the Good Shepherd.**

Prayer of the faithful:

> **For our neophytes (those brought into full communion with us at the Easter Vigil) that they may grow in their likeness to Christ by all they say and do, let us pray to the Lord.**
> **That our candidates and catechumens may come to know and trust Jesus as they continue their faith journey into our parish family, let us pray to the Lord.**

Dismissal based on John 10:11-18.

Fifth Sunday of Easter (B)

[After the proclamation of the gospel or after the homily, the presider says:]

> Would our candidates and catechumens please come forward?

[When they have reached the dismissal area, he walks over to them and dismisses them with these words:]

> My dear candidates and catechumens,
>> today's gospel reading can leave no doubt in our minds
>>> but that we are called to develop
>>> a deep bonding with the Lord Jesus.
>> This gospel challenges all of us
>>> to allow Jesus to live in us.
>> May each of you come to realize more and more
>>> that you can only reach your full potential,
>>> become the beautiful person God intends you to be
>>> and arrive at wholeness, through union with Jesus.
>
> Go now in the peace of Christ
>> to ponder the Scriptures.
>> and break open the Word of God in your lives.

Prayer of the faithful:

> For our neophytes (those brought into full communion with us at the Easter Vigil) that they may experience a sense of belonging to our faith community, let us pray to the Lord.
>
> That our candidates and catechumens may come to realize the importance of being united to Jesus, let us pray to the Lord.

Dismissal based on John 15:1-8.

Sixth Sunday of Easter (B)

[After the proclamation of the gospel or after the homily, the presider says:]

Would our candidates and catechumens please come forward?

[When they have reached the dismissal area, he walks over to them and dismisses them with these words:]

My dear candidates and catechumens,
our Scripture readings for today emphasize
that unselfish love is what makes our lives
meaningful and worth living.
We are challenged by Jesus to love others
as he has loved us.
May you seriously examine your lives
to see the opportunities that are yours
to love unselfishly.

Go now in the peace of Christ
to ponder the Scriptures
and break open the Word of God in your lives.

Prayer of the faithful:

That our neophytes (those brought into full communion with us at the Easter Vigil) may find in the Eucharist a source of strength to love as Jesus loves, let us pray to the Lord.
That our candidates and catechumens experience the joy of loving unselfishly, let us pray to the Lord.

Dismissal based on Acts 10:25-26, 34-35, 44-48; John 15:9-17.

Seventh Sunday of Easter (B)

[After the proclamation of the gospel or after the homily, the presider says:]

> Would our candidates and catechumens please come forward?

[When they have reached the dismissal area, he walks over to them and dismisses them with these words:]

> My dear candidates and catechumens,
>> again this Sunday the Word of God focuses
>>> on the themes of union with God
>>> and our vocation to unselfish love.
>> It is as though we have not been listening to the message
>>> of the Scriptures and so it is repeated.
>> Perhaps in choosing these readings Holy Mother Church
>>> understands how difficult it is for us
>>> to grasp the importance of these concepts:
>>>> growth in a relationship with God
>>>> and living unselfish lives.
>> For this message, my dear friends,
>>> deals with your life here and in eternity.
>
> Go now in the peace of Christ
>> to reflect on the Scriptures
>>> and break open the Word of God in your lives.

Prayer of the faithful:

> For our neophytes (those brought into full communion with us at the Easter Vigil) that they continue to discover in the Eucharist the nourishment needed to live unselfish lives, let us pray to the Lord.
> That our candidates and catechumens may continue to develop a relationship with the Lord and live unselfishly, let us pray to the Lord.

Dismissal based on 1 John 4:11-16; John 17:11-19.

Pentecost (B)

[After the proclamation of the gospel or after the homily, the presider says:]

> **Would our candidates and catechumens please come forward?**

[When they have reached the dismissal area, he walks over to them and dismisses them with these words:]

> **My dear candidates and catechumens,**
> > **like the disciples,**
> > > **we are gathered together as a community in prayer.**
> > > **Even closed doors and fearful hearts**
> > > > **do not hinder God's spirit from reaching us.**
>
> > **May each of you experience the spirit of the Lord**
> > > **working in your lives**
> > > **as you reflect on today's Scriptures.**
>
> > **Go now in the peace of Christ,**
> > > **that peace which he gives to each of you,**
> > > **and be nourished by the Word of God.**
> > > **We look forward to the day when you will gather**
> > > > **with us**
> > > > **to be nourished at the Eucharistic table.**

Prayer of the faithful:

> **For our neophytes, that they may experience the Holy Spirit working in their lives and calling them to ministry, let us pray to the Lord.**
> **That the Holy Spirit may continue to guide our candidates and catechumens and fill their hearts with his love, let us pray to the Lord.**

Dismissal based on the theme of the feast.

Trinity Sunday (B)

[After the proclamation of the gospel or after the homily, the presider says:]

Would our candidates and catechumens please come forward?

[When they have reached the dismissal area, he walks over to them and dismisses them with these words:]

My dear candidates and catechumens,
   in our celebration of Trinity Sunday today,
      we pray that God the Father, God the Son,
      and God the Holy Spirit be revealed to you.
May the God of tenderness, the God of compassion,
      and the God of love and faithfulness
      touch each of your lives.
May you always be open to the mystery
      of the presence and love of the Triune God,
         as you continue your journey of faith
         into full communion with this community.

Go now in the peace of Christ,
      to reflect on the Scriptures
      and break open the Word of God in your lives.

Prayer of the faithful:

For our candidates and catechumens, that they may be ever open to the mystery of the presence and love of the Triune God in their lives, let us pray to the Lord.

Dismissal based on the theme of the feast.

The Body and Blood of Christ (B)

[After the proclamation of the gospel or after the homily, the presider says:]

> Would our candidates and catechumens please come forward?

[When they have reached the dismissal area, he walks over to them and dismisses them with these words:]

> My dear candidates and catechumens,
>> today we celebrate the reality
>>> that the Lord Jesus gave himself to us
>>> under the form of bread and wine.
>
>> May each of you grow in a realization of the
>>> real presence
>>> of the Lord in the Eucharist
>> and come to a better understanding
>>> that in the Eucharist
>>> we are united to the Lord Jesus
>>> and to one another.
>
>> Go now in the peace of Christ
>>> to be nourished by the Word of God.
>>> We look forward to the day when you will gather
>>> with us
>>> to be nourished by Jesus himself in the Eucharist.

Prayer of the faithful:

> That our candidates and catechumens may grow in an appreciation for the sacrament of the Eucharist, let us pray to the Lord.

Dismissal based on John 6:51-58.

Second Sunday of Ordinary Time (B)

[After the proclamation of the gospel or after the homily, the presider says:]

> **Would our candidates and catechumens please come forward?**

[When they have reached the dismissal area, he walks over to them and dismisses them with these words:]

> **My dear candidates and catechumens,**
> > **the Scriptures proclaimed in our midst this Sunday speak to us of listening to the Lord.**
> > **Samuel responds: "Speak, for your servant is** *listening.***"**
> > **While the disciples mentioned in the gospel stay with Jesus for the day; we may wonder what they** *heard* **. . . .**
> > **As a community we are committed to listening to the Lord.**
> > **He says to each of us: "Come and see."**
>
> > **We send you forth to enter into dialogue with the Word of the Lord.**
> > **It is he who will nourish you as you continue your faith journey.**

Prayer of the faithful:

> **For our candidates and catechumens who are also being called by name, that they may listen to what the Lord is asking of them at this point along their faith journey, let us pray to the Lord.**

Dismissal based on 1 Sam 3:3-19; John 1:35-42.

Third Sunday of Ordinary Time (B)

[After the proclamation of the gospel or after the homily, the presider says:]

> **Would our candidates and catechumens please come forward?**

[When they have reached the dismissal area, he walks over to them and dismisses them with these words:]

> **My dear candidates and catechumens,**
> **God's Word is at work in our lives**
> **calling each of us to change—to re-form.**
> **The reign of God—the kingdom—which Jesus brings,**
> **changes our relationships,**
> **our use of possessions,**
> **our standards of what to mourn,**
> **of what to celebrate.**
> **Jesus asks each of you to come after him.**
> **I assure you, my dear friends,**
> **if you will wholeheartedly follow Jesus,**
> **nothing will be untouched in your lives.**
>
> **Go now in the peace of Christ**
> **to ponder the words of Jesus,**
> **to let his challenge nourish your lives.**

Prayer of the faithful:

> **That we, along with our candidates and catechumens,**
> **may have the courage to wholeheartedly follow Jesus,**
> **let us pray to the Lord.**

Dismissal based on Mark 1:14-20.

Fourth Sunday of Ordinary Time (B)

[After the proclamation of the gospel or after the homily, the presider says:]

> Would our candidates and catechumens please come forward?

[When they have reached the dismissal area, he walks over to them and dismisses them with these words:]

> My dear candidates and catechumens,
>> the gospel we have just heard
>>> was not really about someone else, it was about us.
>> And this same Jesus who freed the man
>>> with an unclean spirit, wishes to free each of us
>>>> from any evil that has power over our lives,
>>>> from any barriers that prevent us
>>>>> from following him more closely.
>> May each of us look into our own hearts
>>> and recognize our brokenness, our selfishness,
>>> and be open to Jesus' healing Word.
>
> Go now in the peace of Christ
>> to experience the Word proclaimed here,
>> to let it nourish your own lives.
>> We look forward to the day when you will
>>> gather with us
>>> at the Eucharistic table.

Prayer of the faithful:

> That we, along with our candidates and catechumens, may recognize our brokenness, our selfishness, and be open to Jesus' healing word, let us pray to the Lord.

Dismissal based on Mark 1:21-28.

Fifth Sunday of Ordinary Time (B)

[After the proclamation of the gospel or after the homily, the presider says:]

> Would our candidates and catechumens please come
> forward?

[When they have reached the dismissal area, he walks over to them and dismisses them with these words:]

> My dear candidates and catechumens,
> > today the Scripture readings speak of the brokenhearted,
> > the downtrodden, the sick, and the poor. . . .
> > And we see Jesus' compassion for these people.
> Jesus, through his words and actions,
> > teaches each of us that care for one another
> > and compassion for the unfortunate,
> > are hallmarks of the Christian disciple.
> May the words of the Scriptures take root in your heart
> > and challenge you to a life of compassion and service.
>
> Go now in the peace of Christ
> > to reflect on the Scriptures
> > and break open the Word of God in your lives.

Prayer of the faithful:

> That we, along with our candidates and catechumens,
> may find ways to be compassionate to the broken-
> hearted, the downtrodden, the sick and the poor who
> enter our lives, let us pray to the Lord.

Dismissal based on Job 7:1-4, 6-7; Mark 1:29-39.

Sixth Sunday of Ordinary Time (B)

[After the proclamation of the gospel or after the homily, the presider says:]

Would our candidates and catechumens please come forward?

[When they have reached the dismissal area, he walks over to them and dismisses them with these words:]

My dear candidates and catechumens,
in today's gospel,
the leper who approaches Jesus seeking wholeness
is someone you know.
The ostracized, the helpless, the offensive,
the lonely, the ill,
are the lepers in our lives.
Jesus leads the way to our response to these people.
His compassion sets the example.
May each of you have the courage to see
the lepers in your lives
and respond to them with Christ-like compassion.

Go now in the peace of Christ
to reflect on the Scriptures
and break open the Word of God in your lives.

Prayer of the faithful:

That we, along with our candidates and catechumens,
may have the courage to respond to the people who
need us with Christ-like compassion, let us pray to the
Lord.

Dismissal based on Mark 1:40-45.

Seventh Sunday of Ordinary Time (B)

[After the proclamation of the gospel or after the homily, the presider says:]

Would our candidates and catechumens please come forward?

[When they have reached the dismissal area, he walks over to them and dismisses them with these words:]

**My dear candidates and catechumens,
the Scripture proclaimed in our midst today
tells us of the wonders of our God
who seeks to liberate us from all
that stands in the way of being near him.
May you be open to the Word of God
as it speaks to you.
Let it take root in your hearts
and find expression in your lives.**

**Go now in the peace of Christ
to be nourished on the Word of God.
We look forward to the day when you will gather
with us
to be nourished at the Eucharistic table.**

Prayer of the faithful:

That our candidates and catechumens may continue to draw near to the Lord and experience his care as they continue their faith journey, let us pray to the Lord.

Dismissal based on Isa 43:18-19, 21-22, 24-25; 2 Cor 1:18-22;
Mark 2:1-12.

Eighth Sunday of Ordinary Time (B)

[After the proclamation of the gospel or after the homily, the presider says:]

Would our candidates and catechumens please come forward?

[When they have reached the dismissal area, he walks over to them and dismisses them with these words:]

My dear candidates and catechumens,
it is not unusual for the Scriptures
to present the relationship that exists in marriage
as analogous to the relationship
that God wishes to have with us.
Today's readings do exactly that.
What a joyful concept, to realize that God
really cares for us that much!
As you ponder the Scriptures this morning
may you come to a deeper realization
of God's love for you.

Go now in the peace of Christ
to reflect on the Scriptures
and break open the Word of God in your lives.

Prayer of the faithful:

That our candidates and catechumens may grow in the realization of God's faithful love for them, let us pray to the Lord.

Dismissal based on Hos 2:16-17, 21-22.

Ninth Sunday of Ordinary Time (B)

[After the proclamation of the gospel or after the homily, the presider says:]

> Would our candidates and catechumens please come forward?

[When they have reached the dismissal area, he walks over to them and dismisses them with these words:]

> My dear candidates and catechumens,
>> as you well know, it takes time and effort
>>> to develop a relationship.
>
>> It is the same for our relationship with God
>>> and our relationship with our parish family.
>
>> Each Sunday as we gather here,
>>> our very presence speaks of our need for God
>>> and for the support of one another.
>
>> We are not expected to "go it alone."
>
> May each of you take the time and put forth the effort
>> to become an integral part of your parish family
>>> as we all seek to develop our relationship
>>> with the Lord.
>
> Go now in the peace of Christ
>> to reflect on the Scriptures
>> and break open the Word of God in your lives.

Prayer of the faithful:

> That our candidates and catechumens make our worship together a priority in their lives, let us pray to the Lord.

Dismissal based on Deut 5:12-15; Mark 2:23–3:6.

Tenth Sunday of Ordinary Time (B)

[After the proclamation of the gospel or after the homily, the presider says:]

> **Would our candidates and catechumens please come forward?**

[When they have reached the dismissal area, he walks over to them and dismisses them with these words:]

> **My dear candidates and catechumens,**
> > **we have probably all at sometime in our lives**
> > **experienced the presence of evil.**
> > **Evil is a reality, but through our baptism**
> > > **Christians have the power to overcome it.**
>
> **May you be alert when evil intrudes itself**
> > **into your lives,**
> > **and may you have the courage not to lose heart,**
> > > **but to bring goodness to the situation.**
>
> **Go now in the peace of Christ**
> > **to ponder the Scriptures**
> > **and break open the Word of God in your lives.**

Prayer of the faithful:

> **That our candidates and catechumens may have the courage to overcome evil with goodness, let us pray to the Lord.**

Dismissal based on Gen 3:9-15; 2 Cor 4:13–5:1; Mark 3:20-35.

Eleventh Sunday of Ordinary Time (B)

[After the proclamation of the gospel or after the homily, the presider says:]

Would our candidates and catechumens please come forward?

[When they have reached the dismissal area, he walks over to them and dismisses them with these words:]

My dear candidates and catechumens,
in today's gospel Jesus asks us
what comparison we would make
to express the reign of God.
The answer to that question
depends on what we think the reign of God is.

As you explore the Scriptures this morning
may you grow in your understanding of the reign
of God,
the kingdom of God,
and what it has to do with your life here and now.

Go now in the peace of Christ
to reflect on the Scriptures
and break open the Word of God in your lives.

Prayer of the faithful:

That our candidates and catechumens may grow in their understanding of the reign of God and what it has to do with their lives, let us pray to the Lord.

Dismissal based on Mark 4:26-34.

Twelfth Sunday of Ordinary Time (B)

[After the proclamation of the gospel or after the homily, the presider says:]

> Would our candidates and catechumens please come forward?

[When they have reached the dismissal area, he walks over to them and dismisses them with these words:]

> My dear candidates and catechumens,
>> we all experience stormy times in our lives
>>> and have known our share of destructive elements
>>> which threaten us.
>> In today's Scripture readings
>>> we are presented with accounts of the Lord
>>> stilling the waves.
>
> May you always turn to the Lord in difficult times.
>> Learn to call upon him with trust,
>>> for his power can also be active in your lives.
>
> Go now in the peace of Christ
>> to ponder the Scriptures
>> and break open the Word of God in your lives.

Prayer of the faithful:

> That our candidates and catechumens may trust in the Lord's power when they experience stormy and difficult times in their lives, let us pray to the Lord.

Dismissal based on Job 38:1, 8-11; Mark 4:35-41.

Thirteenth Sunday of Ordinary Time (B)

[After the proclamation of the gospel or after the homily, the presider says:]

> **Would our candidates and catechumens please come forward?**

[When they have reached the dismissal area, he walks over to them and dismisses them with these words:]

> **My dear candidates and catechumens,**
> **our God is a God of life**
> **and he has gifted us with life.**
> **In today's gospel a woman's health**
> **and a child's life are threatened.**
> **Jesus responds to both and liberates them.**
> **May each of you seek Jesus out to liberate you**
> **from the illnesses of our times.**
> **And may you experience Jesus' touch**
> **and his gift of peace in your life.**
>
> **Go now in the peace of Christ**
> **to reflect on the Scriptures**
> **and break open the Word of God in your lives.**

Prayer of the faithful:

> **For our candidates and catechumens, that they may experience Jesus' touch and his gift of peace in their lives, let us pray to the Lord.**

Dismissal based on Mark 5:21-43.

Fourteenth Sunday of Ordinary Time (B)

[After the proclamation of the gospel or after the homily, the presider says:]

> **Would our candidates and catechumens please come forward?**

[When they have reached the dismissal area, he walks over to them and dismisses them with these words:]

> **My dear candidates and catechumens,**
> **today's Scriptures speak of a lack of faith**
> **and a hardness of heart.**
> **We see that a lack of openness**
> **has the power to keep the Lord out of our lives.**
>
> **We pray that each of you continue to be open to the Lord**
> **today and each day, as you journey to full communion**
> **with this faith community.**
>
> **Go now in the peace of Christ**
> **to ponder the Scriptures.**
> **We look forward to the day when you will**
> **gather with us**
> **to be nourished at the Eucharistic table.**

Prayer of the faithful:

> **For our candidates and catechumens, that they may be open to the Lord as they continue their journey into our faith community, let us pray to the Lord.**

Dismissal based on Ezra 2:2-5; Mark 6:1-6.

Fifteenth Sunday of Ordinary Time (B)

[After the proclamation of the gospel or after the homily, the presider says:]

> **Would our candidates and catechumens please come forward?**

[When they have reached the dismissal area, he walks over to them and dismisses them with these words:]

> **My dear candidates and catechumens,**
> > **in today's gospel we see Jesus sending his disciples off.**
> > > **Just so, he has called each of you**
> > > **and he wishes to send you off to**
> > > > **what makes up your daily lives.**
> > **In some way, through you, Jesus wishes**
> > > **to expel demons, anoint the sick,**
> > > **and to work cures.**
> > **Reflect on this sending:**
> > > **What are the demons you need to be rid of?**
> > > **Who are the sick and who need the touch of your care?**
> > > **What are the cures, the healing,**
> > > > **that you can bring about in your own life**
> > > > **and in the lives of others?**
>
> > **Go now and ponder what Jesus may be asking of**
> > > **each of you.**
> > **Reflect on the Scriptures**
> > **and break open the Word of God in your lives.**

Prayer of the faithful:

> **For our candidates and catechumens to realize that Jesus looks to them to continue to bring his presence into the lives of others, let us pray to the Lord.**

Dismissal based on Mark 6:7-13.

Sixteenth Sunday of Ordinary Time (B)

[After the proclamation of the gospel or after the homily, the presider says:]

Would our candidates and catechumens please come forward?

[When they have reached the dismissal area, he walks over to them and dismisses them with these words:]

My dear candidates and catechumens,
our Scripture readings for today
are filled with images of Jesus as the Good Shepherd.
We hear of the compassion Jesus has for us
when we wander far from him,
when we ignore his voice.
Turn to Jesus, the Good Shepherd,
try to draw closer to him this week,
find true rest from all anxieties in him.

Go now in the peace of Christ
to be nourished by the Scriptures
as you prepare to join with us
at the Eucharistic table.

Prayer of the faithful:

For our candidates and catechumens, that they may experience Jesus as the Good Shepherd in their lives, let us pray to the Lord.

Dismissal based on Mark 6:30-34.

Seventeenth Sunday of Ordinary Time (B)

[After the proclamation of the gospel or after the homily, the presider says:]

> Would our candidates and catechumens please come forward?

[When they have reached the dismissal area, he walks over to them and dismisses them with these words:]

> My dear candidates and catechumens,
>> I ask each of you to live a life worthy
>>> of the calling of a Christian:
>>>> with humility, patience, and meekness,
>>>> bearing with others lovingly.
>> For the Lord wishes to touch others
>>> through you this week.
>>> And this, too, is part of the miracle
>>>> of the loaves and fishes!
>
> Go now in the peace of Christ
>> and be nourished by the Word of God.
>
> We look forward to the day when you will join
>> with us
>>> to be nourished with the body and blood of Christ.

Prayer of the faithful:

> For our candidates and catechumens, that their loving kindness may touch the lives of those they meet this week, let us pray to the Lord.

Dismissal based on Eph 4:1-6; John 6:1-15.

Eighteenth Sunday of Ordinary Time (B)

[After the proclamation of the gospel or after the homily, the presider says:]

Would our candidates and catechumens please come forward?

[When they have reached the dismissal area, he walks over to them and dismisses them with these words:]

My dear candidates and catechumens,
it is a joy for this community to have you in our midst!
You remind us of what is ours in the Eucharist,
Jesus, the Bread of Life.
May you find nourishment in the Scripture readings
you share with us each week.
We look forward to the day
when you will also be nourished
on the Bread of Life!

Go now, in the peace of Christ,
to reflect on the Scriptures
and break open the Word of God in your lives.

Prayer of the faithful:

For our candidates and catechumens, that they may experience Jesus in his word, and that he may truly be the Bread of Life for them this week, let us pray to the Lord.

Dismissal based on John 6:24-35.

Nineteenth Sunday of Ordinary Time (B)

[After the proclamation of the gospel or after the homily, the presider says:]

Would our candidates and catechumens please come forward?

[When they have reached the dismissal area, he walks over to them and dismisses them with these words:]

My dear candidates and catechumens,
may you taste and see the goodness of the Lord
as he manifests himself to you in his Word.
The Scriptures of today,
written for the early Christian community,
remind us of our belief in Jesus' presence
in the Eucharist.
May you grow in this faith,
as you prepare to join with us
at the Eucharistic table.

Go now in the peace of Christ
to reflect on the Scriptures
and break open the Word of God in our lives.

Prayer of the faithful:

For our candidates and catechumens, that their faith may grow in the presence of Jesus in the Eucharist, let us pray to the Lord.

Dismissal based on Psalm 34; John 6:41-51.

Twentieth Sunday of Ordinary Time (B)

[After the proclamation of the gospel or after the homily, the presider says:]

> Would our candidates and catechumens please come forward?

[When they have reached the dismissal area, he walks over to them and dismisses them with these words:]

> My dear candidates and catechumens,
>> Jesus gives himself to us as gift in his Word,
>>> proclaimed in our midst,
>>> and in the Eucharist, his body and blood.
>> May you daily experience this Jesus
>>> as he touches you through the Scriptures,
>>> and increases in each of you a longing
>>>> for the gift of himself in the Eucharist.
>> We pray that you may find nourishment in his Word
>>> and we look forward to the day when you will join us
>>>> at the Eucharistic table.
>
> Go now in the peace of Christ
>> to reflect on the Scriptures
>> and break open the Word of God in your lives.

Prayer of the faithful:

> For our candidates and catechumens, that their faith may grow in the presence of Jesus in the Eucharist, let us pray to the Lord.

Dismissal based on John 6:51-58.

Twenty-First Sunday of Ordinary Time (B)

[After the proclamation of the gospel or after the homily, the presider says:]

> **Would our candidates and catechumens please come forward?**

[When they have reached the dismissal area, he walks over to them and dismisses them with these words:]

> **My dear candidates and catechumens,**
>> **today's gospel reading follows on what Jesus said**
>>> **to his disciples last week.**
>> **Our belief in Jesus' presence in the Eucharist**
>>> **is a matter of faith.**
>> **He asks each of us this week:**
>>> **"Do you want to leave me now?"**
>> **May your growing faith in the Eucharist**
>>> **help you to respond**
>>>> **that you also find in Jesus**
>>>>> **the words of eternal life. . . .**
>
> **Go now in the peace of Christ**
>> **to be nourished by the Word of God.**
>> **We look forward to the day when you will join us**
>>> **to be nourished at the Eucharistic banquet.**

Prayer of the faithful:

> **That our candidates and catechumens may have a growing conviction that Jesus nourishes them with his words and will nourish them with his body and blood, let us pray to the Lord.**

Dismissal based on John 6:60-69.

Twenty-Second Sunday of Ordinary Time (B)

[After the proclamation of the gospel or after the homily, the presider says:]

Would our candidates and catechumens please come forward?

[When they have reached the dismissal area, he walks over to them and dismisses them with these words:]

My dear candidates and catechumens,
   in today's gospel Jesus invites each of us to consider:
      that God does not judge us by any external observances
         in which we might be engaged,
      but by the worship which comes from the depths
         of our hearts.

We pray that this gospel message take root in your hearts
   and be a guide to your actions.

Go now in the peace of Christ
   to reflect on the Scriptures
   and break open the Word of God in your lives.

Prayer of the faithful:

For our candidates and catechumens, that the gospel may take root in their lives and be the guide for their actions, let us pray to the Lord.

Dismissal based on Mark 7:1-8, 14-15, 21-23.

Twenty-Third Sunday of Ordinary Time (B)

[After the proclamation of the gospel or after the homily, the presider says:]

> **Would our candidates and catechumens please come forward?**

[When they have reached the dismissal area, he walks over to them and dismisses them with these words:]

> **My dear candidates and catechumens,**
> **Jesus opens the ears of a mute man.**
> **Surely that narrative is our story;**
> **we are that mute person.**
> **Consider the times each of us has been reticent**
> **to speak the good news,**
> **to say the kind word.**
> **Consider the times we have suppressed the kind**
> **or compassionate thought before it reached our lips.**
> **Jesus says *Ephphatha*, that is, "Be opened,"**
> **to each of us this morning.**
> **So let the kind and compassionate words**
> **find a place in your heart**
> **and be spoken on your lips this week.**
>
> **Go now in the peace of Christ**
> **to reflect on the Scriptures**
> **and break open the Word of God in your lives.**

Prayer of the faithful:

> **For our candidates and catechumens, that the kind and compassionate words of the Lord may find a place in their hearts and on their lips, let us pray to the Lord.**

Dismissal based on Mark 7:31-37.

Twenty-Fourth Sunday of Ordinary Time (B)

[After the proclamation of the gospel or after the homily, the presider says:]

> Would our candidates and catechumens please come forward?

[When they have reached the dismissal area, he walks over to them and dismisses them with these words:]

> My dear candidates and catechumens,
>   who is Jesus for you?
>   This is the question that the Scriptures
>   ask each of us today.
>   We are also asked to consider taking up our crosses
>   and following in his steps—
>   even to the point of losing our lives for his sake.
>   We probably find it as difficult to respond
>   as did the disciples.
>   Nevertheless, a response is required.
>
> Go now in the peace of Christ
>   to ponder today's Scriptures
>   and the challenge they present.
>   We look forward to the day when you will join with us
>   at the Eucharistic table.

Prayer of the faithful:

> For our candidates and catechumens, that they may continue to have the courage to accept the path that Jesus points out to them on their faith journey, let us pray to the Lord.

Dismissal based on Mark 8:27-35.

Twenty-Fifth Sunday of Ordinary Time (B)

[After the proclamation of the gospel or after the homily, the presider says:]

> **Would our candidates and catechumens please come forward?**

[When they have reached the dismissal area, he walks over to them and dismisses them with these words:]

> **My dear candidates and catechumens,**
> **may God the Father give to each of you**
> **wisdom from above so that you may grow**
> **in spiritual maturity.**
> **May each of you hear the Lord's call**
> **to be of service to others;**
> **and may the Holy Spirit inspire you to see**
> **how you can be peacemakers**
> **in the conflicts you face.**
>
> **Go now in the peace of Christ**
> **to reflect on the Scriptures**
> **and break open the Word of God in your life.**

Prayer of the faithful:

> **That our candidates and catechumens may grow in spiritual maturity, let us pray to the Lord.**

Dismissal based on Mark 9:30-37.

Twenty-Sixth Sunday of Ordinary Time (B)

[After the proclamation of the gospel or after the homily, the presider says:]

Would our candidates and catechumens please come forward?

[When they have reached the dismissal area, he walks over to them and dismisses them with these words:]

My dear candidates and catechumens,
 today's Scripture readings indicate that
  we have no control of the gifts of the Spirit
   and we need to learn to marvel
    at the Spirit's gifts wherever they are found.
 Where we do have control is in ridding ourselves
  of what hinders the life of the Spirit
   within ourselves.
 The gospel teaches us this message as Jesus
  exaggerates in order to get his point across.
 May each of you look into your own lives,
  marvel at the gifts God has given to you
   and seriously seek to rid yourself
    of whatever hinders you from being Christ-like.

 Go now in the peace of Christ
  to reflect on the Scriptures
  and break open the Word of God in your lives.

Prayer of the faithful:

That our candidates and catechumens may be in touch with God's working in their lives and seek to rid themselves of whatever hinders them from being Christ-like, let us pray to the Lord.

Dismissal based on Num 11:25-29; Mark 9:38-48.

Twenty-Seventh Sunday of Ordinary Time (B)

[After the proclamation of the gospel or after the homily, the presider says:]

Would our candidates and catechumens please come forward?

[When they have reached the dismissal area, he walks over to them and dismisses them with these words:]

My dear candidates and catechumens,
   today's Scriptures bring us into touch
      with God's original design for creation
      and challenge us to be faithful to our commitments.
   Each of us, at one time or another in our lives,
      has experienced broken relationships.
Now we pray that you might forgive yourself
      and others as you seek to be faithful
         to accept the kingdom of God in your lives
         as a gift.

Go now in the peace of Christ
      to reflect on the Scriptures
      and break open the Word of God in your lives.

Prayer of the faithful:

For our candidates and catechumens, that they may experience a healing of the broken relationships in their lives, let us pray to the Lord.

Dismissal based on Gen 2:18-24; Mark 10:2-16.

Twenty-Eighth Sunday of Ordinary Time (B)

[After the proclamation of the gospel or after the homily, the presider says:]

> **Would our candidates and catechumens please come forward?**

[When they have reached the dismissal area, he walks over to them and dismisses them with these words:]

> **My dear candidates and catechumens,**
> > **each of us *is* that man who came running to Jesus.**
> > > **And Jesus looks at each of us with love.**
> > > > **Yet he has a unique way of turning our lives upside down and inside out.**
> > **He asks that you follow him**
> > > **during this stage of your commitment to our Catholic tradition.**
> > > > **What is it that he is asking you to surrender?**
> > **We pray that you have the courage to do "the one thing more"**
> > > **that is asked of you . . . whatever that may be for you.**
>
> > **Go now in the peace of Christ to reflect on the Scriptures and break open the Word of God in your lives.**

Prayer of the faithful:

> **That our candidates and catechumens may be generous in surrendering their lives to Jesus, let us pray to the Lord.**

Dismissal based on Mark 10:17-30.

Twenty-Ninth Sunday of Ordinary Time (B)

[After the proclamation of the gospel or after the homily, the presider says:]

> Would our candidates and catechumens please come forward?

[When they have reached the dismissal area, he walks over to them and dismisses them with these words:]

> My dear candidates and catechumens,
>> you, along with the rest of your parish family
>>> have been challenged today by the call to service.
>> May each of us be convinced that this is what it means
>>> to be a follower of Christ.
>> Daily we are presented with opportunities
>>> to be of service to others.
>> Grasp the opportunity!
>>> Christ will be there to support and guide you
>>> in your efforts to follow him.
>
> Go now in the peace of Christ
>> to reflect on the challenge of today's Scriptures
>> and to break open the Word of God in your lives.
>> We look forward to the day when you will join us
>>> at the Eucharistic table.

Prayer of the faithful:

> For our candidates and catechumens, that they may accept the challenge that Jesus gives to his followers, placing themselves at the service of others, let us pray to the Lord.

Dismissal based on Mark 10:35-45.

Thirtieth Sunday of Ordinary Time (B)

[After the proclamation of the gospel or after the homily, the presider says:]

> Would our candidates and catechumens please come forward?

[When they have reached the dismissal area, he walks over to them and dismisses them with these words:]

> My dear candidates and catechumens,
>> each of us is the blind beggar Bartimaeus,
>>> and it is Jesus who comes to offer us sight.
>> Our Catholic faith tradition gives us a sight and vision
>>> that goes far beyond the physical power to see.
>> We pray that you may see the meaning
>>> in the incomprehensible situations of your lives.
>>> May you, like Bartimaeus, experience the healing
>>>> which Jesus alone can give.
>
>> Go now in the peace of Christ
>>> and be nourished by the Scriptures.
>>> We look forward to the day when you will gather
>>>> with us
>>>> at the Eucharistic table.

Prayer of the faithful:

> That our candidates and catechumens may experience the sight and vision that Jesus brings into their lives, let us pray to the Lord.

Dismissal based on Mark 10:46-52.

Thirty-First Sunday of Ordinary Time (B)

[After the proclamation of the gospel or after the homily, the presider says:]

> **Would our candidates and catechumens please come forward?**

[When they have reached the dismissal area, he walks over to them and dismisses them with these words:]

> **My dear candidates and catechumens,**
> > **in today's Scripture readings you have heard,**
> > > **along with us,**
> > > **that the important thing to do in our lives**
> > > **is to love.**
> > **It is for each of you to understand, to balance,**
> > **and develop all three loves**
> > **within our Catholic faith tradition:**
> > > **love of God,**
> > > **a selfless love of neighbor,**
> > > **and a love for yourselves.**
>
> **Go now in the peace of Christ**
> > **to reflect on the Scriptures**
> > **and to break open the Word of God in your lives.**

Prayer of the faithful:

> **For our candidates and catechumens, that they may grow in an understanding of the importance of love in their lives, let us pray to the Lord.**

Dismissal based on Mark 12:28-34.

Thirty-Second Sunday of Ordinary Time (B)

[After the proclamation of the gospel or after the homily, the presider says:]

Would our candidates and catechumens please come forward?

[When they have reached the dismissal area, he walks over to them and dismisses them with these words:]

My dear candidates and catechumens,
   today's Scripture readings ask us to explore
      the meaning of giving everything,
      the meaning of surrendering.
Jesus alone knows the gift of yourself
      which you bring to our parish family.
      We are grateful that you have come to us
         and we support you with our prayers
         as you continue your faith journey.

Go now in the peace of Christ
      to be nourished by the Scriptures
      and to break open the Word of God in your lives.

Prayer of the faithful:

That we, the parish family, may appreciate the candidates and catechumens who come to us, wishing to share our faith tradition, and that we may remember them before the Lord, let us pray to the Lord.

Dismissal based on 1 Kgs 17:10-16; Mark 12:38-44.

Thirty-Third Sunday of Ordinary Time (B)

[After the proclamation of the gospel or after the homily, the presider says:]

Would our candidates and catechumens please come forward?

[When they have reached the dismissal area, he walks over to them and dismisses them with these words:]

**My dear candidates and catechumens,
  the Scripture readings proclaimed in our midst
      this morning
    were all written during times of persecution.
We are to understand from them that Christ
    will triumph over evil on the last day.
Like the early Christians who listened to the gospel,
    you, too, experience your own periods
      of crisis and doubt.
I assure you that Christ is with you.
    Turn to him for reassurance
      when your journey is difficult.
    He will never fail you
      for he triumphs over evil!**

**Go now in the peace of Christ
    to reflect on the Scriptures.
    We support you with our prayers.**

Prayer of the faithful:

That our candidates and catechumens may rely on Christ when they experience periods of crisis and doubt, let us pray to the Lord.

Dismissal based on Mark 13:24-32.

Feast of Christ the King (B)

[After the proclamation of the gospel or after the homily, the presider says:]

> Would our candidates and catechumens please come forward?

[When they have reached the dismissal area, he walks over to them and dismisses them with these words:]

> My dear candidates and catechumens,
>> today is the feast of Christ the King
>>> and the gospel reading focuses our attention
>>>> on leadership.
>> May you come to an understanding that the leadership
>>> that Christ has to offer us is one
>>> that is orientated toward the good of all.
>> We pray that you may experience his leadership
>>> in your life, and that you have the courage
>>>> to follow the Lord wherever he may lead you.
>
> Go now in the peace of Christ
>> to be nourished by the hope that today's Scriptures
>>> offer us.
>> We look forward to the day when you will gather
>>> with us
>>> at the Eucharistic table.

Prayer of the faithful:

> For our candidates and catechumens, that they may have the courage to follow the Lord wherever he may lead them, let us pray to the Lord.

Dismissal based on John 18:33-37.

First Sunday of Advent (C)

[After the proclamation of the gospel or after the homily, the presider says:]

Would our candidates and catechumens please come forward?

[When they have reached the dismissal area, he walks over to them and dismisses them with these words:]

My dear candidates and catechumens,
 today we begin a new liturgical year
  with the season of Advent.
 This is a time for us when we look for the
   Lord's comings:
  he comes to us each day
   in a variety of disguises.
    Advent is a time to learn
     to recognize his many comings into our lives.
 Wait patiently and prayerfully for his coming . . .
  for he will surely come!

 Go now in the peace of Christ
  to be nourished on the Scriptures
  and break open the Word of God in your lives.

Prayer of the faithful:

For our candidates and catechumens, that they may learn to recognize the Lord as he comes into their lives this Advent, let us pray to the Lord.

Dismissal based on the theme of the Advent season.

Second Sunday of Advent (C)

[After the proclamation of the gospel or after the homily, the presider says:]

Would our candidates and catechumens please come forward?

[When they have reached the dismissal area, he walks over to them and dismisses them with these words:]

My dear candidates and catechumens,
Advent is a season of preparation,
not just a preparation to celebrate Christmas
but a time to take a look at our lives
and to prepare a clear way for the Lord.
And so I now ask each of you to consider:
What paths in your lives do you need to straighten?
What valleys do you need to fill?
What mountains need to be leveled?
What winding ways need to be made straight
and what rough ways need to be made smooth?
This is the work of your preparation
as you journey through Advent.
Your parish community now sends you forth
to reflect upon the Word of God
which you have shared with us this morning.
Be assured of our loving support and prayers
throughout this Advent season.

Prayer of the faithful:

That we, along with our candidates and catechumens, may experience the nearness of the Lord during this Advent and learn to value the things that really matter, let us pray to the Lord.

Dismissal based on Luke 3:1-6.

Third Sunday of Advent (C)

[After the proclamation of the gospel or after the homily, the presider says:]

> Would our candidates and catechumens please come forward?

[When they have reached the dismissal area, he walks over to them and dismisses them with these words:]

> My dear candidates and catechumens,
>   today's Scripture readings remind us
>   that the Lord is near.
>   He has entered into our history.
>   He has entered into your life story,
>   and the question of the gospel:
>   "What are we to do?"
>   offers a challenge to all of us.
>
> Go now in the peace of Christ
>   to be nourished by the Scriptures,
>   their words of comfort and challenge,
>   as you continue your journey with us through Advent.
>   We long for the day when the Lord will come to you
>   in the Eucharist.

Prayer of the faithful:

> For our candidates and catechumens, that they may find comfort, challenge, and nourishment as they reflect on today's Scriptures, let us pray to the Lord.

Dismissal based on Zeph 3:14-18; Luke 3:10-18.

Fourth Sunday of Advent (C)

[After the proclamation of the gospel or after the homily, the presider says:]

> **Would our candidates and catechumens please come forward?**

[When they have reached the dismissal area, he walks over to them and dismisses them with these words:]

> **My dear candidates and catechumens,**
>   **the Scriptures proclaimed in our midst this morning**
>   **all speak of the Lord's coming**
>   **and the *unexpected ways that he comes*.**
>   **This same Lord also continues to come among us**
>   ***in unexpected ways*.**
>   **May each of you recognize him in the unexpected,**
>   **as you continue your journey with us through Advent.**
>
> **My dear friends, go now to reflect on today's Scriptures**
>   **and break open the Word of God in your lives.**
>   **We long for the day when the Lord will come to you**
>   **in the Eucharist.**

Prayer of the faithful:

> **That we, along with our candidates and catechumens,**
> **may learn to recognize the Lord in the unexpected**
> **events of our lives, let us pray to the Lord.**

Dismissal based on Mic 5:1-4; Heb 10:5-10; Luke 1:39-45.

Christmas (C)

[After the proclamation of the gospel or after the homily, the presider says:]

> **Would our candidates and catechumens please come forward?**

[When they have reached the dismissal area, he walks over to them and dismisses them with these words:]

> **My dear candidates and catechumens,**
>   **we wish you the joy of this day!**
> **May your reflections on today's Scriptures**
>   **help you reach the conviction**
>   **that light overcomes darkness**
>   **and that each of you is called**
>   **to experience his enduring love.**
>
> **Go now to be nourished by the Word of God,**
>   **his gift to us.**
> **We long for the day when you will experience**
>   **the Lord's presence in the Eucharist.**

Prayer of the faithful:

> **That our candidates and catechumens may experience the enduring love of the Lord in their lives, let us pray to the Lord.**

Dismissal based on John 1:1-18.

Holy Family (C)

[After the proclamation of the gospel or after the homily, the presider says:]

Would our candidates and catechumens please come forward?

[When they have reached the dismissal area, he walks over to them and dismisses them with these words:]

My dear candidates and catechumens,
   we find ourselves celebrating the feast of the
      Holy Family
   within the Christmas season, because it is a celebration
      of the presence of Jesus among us.
May your relationships within your own families
   be guided by the virtues presented in the reading:
      the virtues of compassion, kindness, humility,
      patience, forgiveness, and love.
May the love that binds you to your families
   extend beyond them to those who need
   your patience, forgiveness, and love.

   Go now in the peace of Christ
   to reflect on the Scriptures
   and break open the Word of God in your lives.

Prayer of the faithful:

That our candidates and catechumens may experience our love and concern for them and that they may share the love of Jesus with others, let us pray to the Lord.

Dismissal based on Col 3:12-21.

Mother of God (C)

[After the proclamation of the gospel or after the homily, the presider says:]

Would our candidates and catechumens please come forward?

[When they have reached the dismissal area, he walks over to them and dismisses them with these words:]

My dear candidates and catechumens,
on this feast of Mary, the Mother of God,
I pray that each of you may experience
the graciousness of our God.
Like Mary, may you treasure those times
when God makes himself known to you
and reflect upon his presence in your lives.

Go now in the peace of Christ
to be nourished on the Scriptures
and break open the Word of God in your lives.

Prayer of the faithful:

That our candidates and catechumens may find in Mary, the Mother of God, a model for their own spiritual lives, let us pray to the Lord.
For those who minister to our candidates and catechumens, that they may continue to manifest the Church's loving call to those new members of our faith community, let us pray to the Lord.

Dismissal based on Num 6:22-27; Luke 2:16-21.

Second Sunday after Christmas (C)

[After the proclamation of the gospel or after the homily, the presider says:]

> Would our candidates and catechumens please come
> forward?

[When they have reached the dismissal area, he walks over to them and dismisses them with these words:]

> My dear candidates and catechumens,
> > the Letter to the Ephesians which we have just heard
> > > expresses our sentiments this morning:
> > > we thank God for you and pray for you,
> > > > that you may know more clearly the Lord Jesus
> > > > and the love that he has for you.
> > May your innermost vision be so clarified
> > > that you see how he is calling each of you
> > > into his own likeness.
> > For that is your glorious heritage!
>
> > Go now in the peace of Christ
> > > to reflect on the Scriptures and the heritage
> > > that is yours in Christ Jesus, our Lord.

Prayer of the faithful:

> That our candidates and catechumens may experience
> in this community the wealth of their Catholic heritage
> and a sense of the hope that is theirs as they continue
> their faith journey, let us pray to the Lord.

Dismissal based on Eph 1:3-6, 15-18.

Epiphany (C)

[After the proclamation of the gospel or after the homily, the presider says:]

Would our candidates and catechumens please come forward?

[When they have reached the dismissal area, he walks over to them and dismisses them with these words:]

My dear candidates and catechumens,
   today we celebrate the feast of Epiphany,
     the manifestation of Christ to all peoples.
In the journey of the kings, we recall our own journey,
     as the same Lord leads us out of darkness
     and even accompanies us along the way.
Our prayer is for you to persevere in your faith journey,
     to be open and ready to offer your gifts to God.

Go now in the peace of Christ
   to reflect on the Scriptures
   and be nourished by the Word of God.
We look forward to the day when your journey
     will bring you to the Eucharistic table.

Prayer of the faithful:

That our candidates and catechumens may find our parish family a light to them on their journey into the fullness of our faith community, let us pray to the Lord.

Dismissal based on Matt 2:1-12.

Baptism of the Lord (C)

[After the proclamation of the gospel or after the homily, the presider says:]

> Would our candidates and catechumens please come forward?

[When they have reached the dismissal area, he walks over to them and dismisses them with these words:]

> My dear candidates and catechumens,
>> today's feast, the Baptism of the Lord,
>> brings to a close the liturgical season of Christmastide.
> The Scripture readings stimulate reflection
>> on the whole purpose of Christ's coming among us,
>> and how in baptism we also become God's
>>> favored ones.
> You are already "beloved" by God.
>> Don't miss a chance to live out your calling
>> as his sons and daughters:
>>> be faithful in prayer and loving in action.
> His favor rests on each of you.
>> Now it is up to you to activate that favor
>> in your regard.
>
> Go now in the peace of Christ
>> to reflect on the Scriptures
>> and break open the Word of God in your lives.

Prayer of the faithful:

> That our candidates and catechumens may be faithful
> to their call and may experience the support of this
> baptized community, let us pray to the Lord.

Dismissal based on Luke 3:15-16, 21-22.

First Sunday of Lent (C)

[At the end of the Rite of Sending, the presider addresses the following words to the candidates and catechumens as their dismissal:]

And so, my dear Elect,
in the name of this parish family, I now send you
(Names of the Elect are inserted here.)
to your cathedral this evening
to be joined by other catechumens who are seeking
baptism in our faith,
and other candidates who are seeking
full communion in the Catholic community.
[The presider extends his hands over the Elect.]
You have been chosen by God
and have entered with us into this way of Lent.
May Christ Jesus himself
teach you the value of prayer and fasting
in meeting temptation,
especially during this time of Lenten retreat.

Go now in peace. Soon you will join with us
to be nourished at the Eucharistic table.

Prayer of the faithful:

That all candidates and catechumens may experience
the universality and love of our Catholic faith tradition
as they meet with the bishop for the Rite of Election,
let us pray to the Lord.

Dismissal based on Luke 4:1-13.

Optional Dismissal for First Sunday of Lent (C)

(To be used when the Rite of Sending does not take place.)

[After the proclamation of the gospel or after the homily, the presider says:]

> **Would our candidates and catechumens please come forward?**

[When they have reached the dismissal area, he walks over to them and dismisses them with these words:]

> **My dear candidates and catechumens,**
> > **you gather with us today as we begin the season of Lent.**
> **With Jesus each of us is led into the desert**
> > **to be liberated from the compulsions of the world**
> > **and to open our hearts to the kingdom of God.**
> **We invite you to join with us**
> > **in prayer, in fasting, and in almsgiving,**
> > > **three ways through which God**
> > > **makes his presence known to us.**
>
> **Go now in the peace of Christ**
> > **to reflect on the Scriptures**
> > **and break open the Word of God in your lives.**
> **We long for the day when you will join with us**
> > **to be nourished at the Eucharistic table.**

Prayer of the faithful:

> **That our candidates and catechumens may be open to the inspirations of the Spirit, let us pray to the Lord.**

Dismissal based on theme of the Lenten season.

Second Sunday of Lent (C)

[After the proclamation of the gospel or after the homily, the presider says:]

Would our Elect please come forward?

[When they have reached the dismissal area, he walks over to them and dismisses them with these words:]

My dear Elect,
may you take as your guide
during this Lenten period
the example of Jesus:
a Jesus who takes time for prayer,
a Jesus who accepts the cross.
Our prayer for you
is that you stand firm in the Lord.
This I believe you will do if you will truly listen to him.

Go now in the peace of Christ.
Accept the cross in your life this week;
take time to be with the Lord in prayer.
We look forward to your joining with us
at the Eucharistic table.

Prayer of the faithful:

That our candidates and catechumens may stand firm in the Lord, accepting the cross as the way of the Christian, and take the time to listen to the Lord in daily prayer.

Dismissal based on Phil 3:17–4:1; Luke 9:28-36.

Optional Dismissal for Second Sunday of Lent (C)
(To be used when there are no Elect.)

[After the proclamation of the gospel or after the homily, the presider says:]

> **Would our candidates and catechumens please come forward?**

[When they have reached the dismissal area, he walks over to them and dismisses them with these words:]

> **My dear candidates and catechumens,**
>   **may the light of the transfigured Lord**
>   **shine upon each of you**
>   **and relieve you of any fear or holding back**
>   **on your faith journey.**
>   **May you be transformed into the likeness of Jesus**
>   **as you continue to experience the Lenten season.**
>
> **Go now in the peace of Christ**
>   **to reflect on the Scriptures**
>   **and break open the Word of God in your lives.**

Prayer of the faithful:

> **For our candidates and catechumens, that they may be open to the ways in which Jesus wishes to transform their lives, let us pray to the Lord.**

Dismissal based on Luke 9:28-36.

Third Sunday of Lent (C)

[The great conversion stories are used for the Scrutinies. These are the readings of cycle A and they are used no matter what the current cycle is. At the end of the First Scrutiny the presider addresses the Elect:]

My dear Elect,
   your experience and our experience
      has been that of the Samaritan woman.
   Now may we seek from Jesus
      living water:
         a water which will help us see ourselves
            for who we really are,
         a water which will satisfy our deepest longings.
   We send you forth to reflect on your experience
      and continue to be nourished by the Word of God.

Go now in the peace of Christ.
   We eagerly await the day when you will
      partake with us
   of the Eucharistic banquet.

Prayer of the faithful:

That our Elect may experience Jesus as the living water, refreshing them throughout their faith journey, let us pray to the Lord.

Dismissal based on John 4:5-42.

Optional Dismissal for Third Sunday of Lent (C)

(To be used when there are no Elect.)

[After the proclamation of the gospel or after the homily, the presider says:]

> **Would our candidates and catechumens please come forward?**

[When they have reached the dismissal area, he walks over to them and dismisses them with these words:]

> **My dear candidates and catechumens,**
> > **the images in today's Scriptures**
> > > **speak to us of God's presence:**
> > > > **the burning bush, the cloud, the vine dresser,**
> > > > **and of his desire to nourish us.**
> > **Now it is up to us during this Lenten period**
> > > **to discern the presence of the Lord each day**
> > > **and to bear fruit by our Christ-like lives.**
>
> **Go now in the peace of Christ**
> > **to explore the images of God's presence**
> > > **in today's Scriptures**
> > > **and to discover his presence in your lives.**

Prayer of the faithful:

> **That our candidates and catechumens may discover the Lord's presence in their own lives and be nourished by the Word of God as they journey into this faith community.**

Dismissal based on Exod 3:1-8, 13-15; 1 Cor 10:1-6, 10-12;
        Luke 13:1-9.

Fourth Sunday of Lent (C)

[At the end of the Second Scrutiny, the presider addresses the Elect:]

> And now, my dear Elect,
>> until we meet again at the next scrutiny,
>>> go in peace,
>>>> and may he who is the Light of the World
>>>> be with each of you.
>
> We send you forth to reflect on the account
>> of the man born blind,
>> and how that person is you.
> May you be nourished by the Word of God
>> made present in your lives.
> Your whole parish family longs to have you join with us
>> at the banquet of the Eucharist.

Prayer of the faithful:

> For our Elect, that they may truly experience the Lord opening their eyes to a Christian vision of the world, let us pray to the Lord.

Dismissal based on John 9:1-41.

Optional Dismissal for Fourth Sunday of Lent (C)

(To be used when there are no Elect.)

[After the proclamation of the gospel or after the homily, the presider says:]

> **Would our candidates and catechumens please come forward?**

[When they have reached the dismissal area, he walks over to them and dismisses them with these words:]

> **My dear candidates and catechumens,**
> > **today's Scripture readings seem to celebrate arrivals—**
> > **having made it.**
> **At times we seem to lose sight of**
> > **where we are going and why.**
> > **That is one of the reasons we need companions**
> > > **on our journey—people who will**
> > > **accept and encourage us.**
> **May each of you know that we pray for you**
> > **during your faith journey into our community.**
> **A merciful Father, according to this morning's parable,**
> > **awaits your arriving home.**
>
> **Go now in the peace of Christ**
> > **to be nourished by the Word of God.**
> > **We look forward to the day when you will join us**
> > > **at the Eucharistic celebration.**

Prayer of the faithful:

> **That our candidates and catechumens may have the courage to offer forgiveness and acceptance to those who seem to be unworthy of it, let us pray to the Lord.**

Dismissal based on Josh 5:9, 10-12; 2 Cor 5:17-21; Luke 15:1-3, 11-32.

Fifth Sunday of Lent (C)

[At the end of the Third Scrutiny the presider addresses the Elect:]

My dear friends,
the Lord Jesus raised Lazarus from the dead
as a sign that he had come
to give us life in full measure.
May he rescue you, our Elect,
from all death-dealing situations
as you seek life in the sacraments.
By his Holy Spirit,
may he fill each of you with new life,
increasing your faith, hope, and love,
so that you may have life to the fullest
and thus come to share in his resurrection.

My dear Elect,
we now send you forth to reflect more deeply
upon the Word of God
and the events which we have shared today.

Prayer of the faithful:

For our Elect, that they may learn to trust in the Lord
and his power in the death-dealing situations of their
own lives, let us pray to the Lord.

Dismissal based on John 11:1-45.

Optional Dismissal for Fifth Sunday of Lent (C)

(To be used when there are no Elect.)

[After the proclamation of the gospel or after the homily, the presider says:]

> Would our candidates and catechumens please come forward?

[When they have reached the dismissal area, he walks over to them and dismisses them with these words:]

> My dear candidates and catechumens,
>> today's Scripture readings invite us
>>> to be optimistic about our futures.
>> Ours is a merciful God,
>>> who is less interested in our past,
>>> and whose emphasis is on the future which Christ
>>>> has already won for us.
>> May you experience that the Lord
>>> is doing something new in you
>>> during this grace-filled season of Lent.
>
>> Go now in the peace of Christ
>>> to reflect on the Scriptures
>>> and break open the Word of God in your lives.

Prayer of the faithful:

> That our candidates and catechumens believe in God's merciful love, let us pray to the Lord.

Dismissal based on Isa 43:16-21; Phil 3:8-14; John 8:1-11.

Passion/Palm Sunday (C)

[After the proclamation of the gospel or after the homily, the presider says:]

Would our Elect please come forward?

[When they have reached the dismissal area, he walks over to them and dismisses them with these words:]

My dear Elect,
　　you join with us today to begin
　　　the most solemn week of the year.
　Holy Mother Church extends to each of you
　　　the many graces and blessings of this holy week.
　I ask that you now continue your preparation
　　by reflecting on God's Word:
　　　consider Christ's attitude,
　　　pray that his attitude becomes more your own.

　Go forth now to be nourished by the Scriptures.
　We look forward to your joining with us
　as we celebrate Holy Thursday and Good Friday.
　We, too, long for the Holy Saturday Vigil,
　　when you will celebrate with us in fullness.

Prayer of the faithful:

For our Elect as they begin their final preparations for baptism and full communion with this Catholic faith community at the Easter Vigil, let us pray to the Lord.

Dismissal based on Phil 2:6-11.

Optional Dismissal for Passion/Palm Sunday (C)
(To be used when there are no Elect.)

[After the proclamation of the gospel or after the homily, the presider says:]

> Would our candidates and catechumens please come
> forward?

[When they have reached the dismissal area, he walks over to them and dismisses them with these words:]

> My dear candidates and catechumens,
>> Jesus identifies himself with us
>>> through his death on the cross.
>> He willingly faces the gravest of our fears—
>>> annihilation.
>> He has identified himself with us.
>>> Now it is up to each of you to ponder
>>> on how you have identified yourself with him
>>>> throughout your Lenten journey.
>
> Go now in the peace of Christ
>> to reflect on the Scriptures
>> and break open the Word of God in your lives.

Prayer of the faithful:

> That through their Lenten journey, our candidates and
> catechumens become more Christ-like, let us pray to
> the Lord.

Dismissal based on theme of the Sunday.

Holy Thursday—Presentation of the Our Father with Dismissal (C)

[After the proclamation of the gospel or after the homily, the presider says:]

Would our Elect please come forward?

[When they have reached the dismissal area, he walks over to them and continues with these words:]

My dear friends,
on this evening Catholics throughout the world
remember that our Lord Jesus gave us himself
under the form of bread and wine,
for nourishment on our spiritual journey.

Soon you, my dear Elect,
will be joining us at the Eucharistic banquet.
At that time you will pray the prayer with us
that Jesus himself entrusted to his disciples.

Since antiquity this prayer has been part of our
Communion rite—the praying together by the
entire community of the Our Father.

In the Our Father we pray: "Thy kingdom come."
That kingdom is not just something in the future;
it is involved in the here and now
as we minister to one another.

[Presider now blesses the prayer card or missal and hands it to each of the Elect. If the individual has already been baptized in another faith tradition he says:]

(Name of individual/s), you have known this prayer
through your previous faith tradition.

We ask that you now pray it often during these
   final days of preparation
      for the day you will pray it with us
      and be nourished by the Eucharist,
      the body and blood of the Lord Jesus.

[If the individual has not been baptized, he says:]

(Name of individual/s), we are happy to share
   with you
   our ancient heritage of faith and prayer.
We ask that you now pray the Our Father
   often during these coming days
      as you prepare for the day
      you will pray it with us
         and be nourished by the Eucharist,
         the body and blood of the Lord Jesus.

[The presider now touches/embraces each of the Elect and says:]

My dear Elect,
   we send you forth from our midst lovingly
      so you may ponder
         what you have seen,
         what you have heard,
         and what you have experienced this evening.
   Our prayers go with you
      as you prepare to join us
      at the Eucharistic banquet
         during the Easter Vigil.

Prayer of the faithful:

For our Elect, that they may have a living faith in the
Eucharistic presence of Jesus, let us pray to the Lord.

Dismissal based on the theme of the Our Father.

Good Friday—Presentation of the Creed with Dismissal (C)

[After the veneration of the cross, the presider says:]

Would our Elect please come forward?

[When they have reached the dismissal area, he walks over to them and continues with these words:]

You, my dear Elect,
have entered into our remembering
of the Lord's passion and death.

This memory is part of our profession of faith.
In the Nicene Creed, which we pray each Sunday,
Catholics profess:

"For our sake he was crucified,
under Pontius Pilate;
he suffered, died, and was buried."

[The presider now blesses the prayer card or missal and hands it to each of the Elect. If the individual has already been baptized in another faith tradition he says:]

(Name of individual/s), the Creed has been a part of
your religious tradition and has nurtured your faith
throughout the years.

Now, we, your Catholic faith community,
hand it over to you anew,
asking that you once again accept this statement
of belief.

[If the individual has not been baptized, he says:]

(Name of individual/s), this is the statement of our
faith.

It is a precious part of our heritage
which we, as your parish family,
entrust to you
   as you begin your final preparation
   for baptism and full sacramental life
      as a Catholic.

We now ask that you accept it
   as your profession of faith.

[The presider now touches/embraces each of the Elect and says:]

We lovingly send you forth from this community
   to ponder what you have heard,
   what you have seen,
   and what you have experienced this evening.

Take with you your Creed.
   Our prayers go with you as you prepare
   to join with us at the Eucharistic table
      this Easter Vigil.

Prayer of the faithful:

That our Elect, along with the Elect throughout the
world, may allow the death of the Lord to touch their
personal lives, we pray to the Lord.

Dismissal based on the presentation of the Creed.

Easter Sunday (C)

(This dismissal is only used if there are candidates and catechumens present. The neophytes remain for the entire liturgy.)

[After the proclamation of the gospel or after the homily, the presider says:]

> **Would our candidates and catechumens please come forward?**

[When they have reached the dismissal area, he walks over to them and dismisses them with these words:]

> **My dear candidates and catechumens,**
>> **let us celebrate the joy of the Risen Lord this Easter.**
>>> **May you dare to trust**
>>>> **that God has affirmed**
>>>> **all that you hope for . . . and much more.**
>
>> **May you live this week joyfully**
>>> **in the embrace of the Risen Lord.**
>
>> **Go now in the peace of Christ**
>>> **to ponder on the Scriptures**
>>> **and break open the Word of God in your lives.**

Prayer of the faithful:

> **For our neophytes, those who were baptized and brought into full communion with our faith community at the Easter Vigil, that they may worship with us in joy, let us pray to the Lord.**
> **For our candidates and catechumens, that they may more deeply trust in the Lord and experience the joy that he alone can give them, let us pray to the Lord.**

Dismissal based on the theme of the feast.

185

Second Sunday of Easter (C)

[After the proclamation of the gospel or after the homily, the presider says:]

> **Would our candidates and catechumens please come forward?**

[When they have reached the dismissal area, he walks over to them and dismisses them with these words:]

> **My dear candidates and catechumens,**
> **as we celebrate the joy of the Risen Lord this Eastertide,**
> **may you experience the peace of the Risen Christ,**
> **his gift to each of you.**
>
> **This community now sends you forth**
> **to reflect more deeply on the Word of God**
> **which you have shared with us this morning.**
> **Be assured of our loving support and prayers for you.**
> **We look forward to the day**
> **when you will share fully with us**
> **at the Eucharistic table.**

Prayer of the faithful:

> **For our neophytes, those brought into full communion with us at the Easter Vigil, that they may experience a joyful peace in their lives, let us pray to the Lord.**
> **For our candidates and catechumens, that they may grow in faith and make their own the words of Thomas: "My Lord and my God," we pray to the Lord.**

Dismissal based on John 20:19-31.

Third Sunday of Easter (C)

[After the proclamation of the gospel or after the homily, the presider says:]

> Would our candidates and catechumens please come forward?

[When they have reached the dismissal area, he walks over to them and dismisses them with these words:]

> My dear candidates and catechumens,
>> the victorious Lord is always with us
>>> and today's Scripture readings encourage us
>>>> to recognize him.
>> The disciples recognized him
>>> through their successful fishing trip,
>>> and they *knew* it was the Lord
>>>> in the breaking of the bread.
>> May you also recognize Jesus, hear him,
>>> and learn to take his advice.
>
> Go now in the peace of Christ
>> to reflect on the Scriptures
>> and break open the Word of God in your lives.

Prayer of the faithful:

> For our neophytes, those baptized and brought into full communion with us at the Easter Vigil, that they may recognize the Lord in the breaking of the bread, let us pray to the Lord.
>> May our candidates and catechumens come to recognize Jesus as he accompanies them on their faith journey, let us pray to the Lord.

Dismissal based on Acts 5:27-32, 40-41; Rev 5:11-14; John 21:1-19.

Fourth Sunday of Easter (C)

[After the proclamation of the gospel or after the homily, the presider says:]

> **Would our candidates and catechumens please come forward?**

[When they have reached the dismissal area, he walks over to them and dismisses them with these words:]

> **My dear candidates and catechumens,**
> > **the Lord Jesus is our Good Shepherd**
> > > **who helps those who place their trust in him.**
> > **May each of you recognize his voice**
> > > **so that you may live in the confidence**
> > **of his daily care for you**
> > > **and may follow him**
> > > > **to the fullness of eternal life.**
>
> > **Go now in the peace of Christ**
> > > **and be nourished on the Word of God.**
> > **Be assured of our loving support and prayers for you**
> > > **as we look forward to the day**
> > > **when you will join us to be nourished**
> > > > **at the Eucharistic table.**

Prayer of the faithful:

> **For our neophytes, those brought into full communion with us at the Easter Vigil, that they may continue to experience the power of the Risen Lord working in their lives, let us pray to the Lord.**
> **For our candidates and catechumens, that they may believe in God's great love for them as they break open the Word of the Lord and reflect on its meaning in their lives, let us pray to the Lord.**

Dismissal based on John 10:27-30.

Fifth Sunday of Easter (C)

[After the proclamation of the gospel or after the homily, the presider says:]

> Would our candidates and catechumens please come forward?

[When they have reached the dismissal area, he walks over to them and dismisses them with these words:]

> My dear candidates and catechumens,
> > what a challenge we find in the closing words
> > > of today's gospel:
> > > > seeing how we love one another
> > > > is how people will know that we are followers
> > > > > of Jesus.
> > To a person looking at your lifestyle,
> > > are you recognizable as a follower of Jesus?
> > The Lord's kingdom has begun in us.
> > > May you join with us in helping that kingdom come!
>
> Go now in the peace of Christ
> > to be nourished by the Word of God,
> > to make it your own,
> > and let it form you into the image of Christ.

Prayer of the faithful:

> For our neophytes, those brought into full communion with us at the Easter Vigil, that they may be recognized as followers of Jesus by their unselfish love, let us pray to the Lord.
> That our candidates and catechumens may have the courage this week to find ways of expressing an unselfish love, let us pray to the Lord.

Dismissal based on Acts 14:21-27; Rev 21:1-5; John 13:31-35.

Sixth Sunday of Easter (C)

[After the proclamation of the gospel or after the homily, the presider says:]

Would our candidates and catechumens please come forward?

[When they have reached the dismissal area, he walks over to them and dismisses them with these words:]

My dear candidates and catechumens,
 guided by the Spirit,
  the gift of the Risen Jesus
   to his disciples,
    we are daily reminded of all that Jesus
     shared with us.
May the same Spirit
 help each of you experience
 the peace that Jesus has given us
  as his farewell gift.

Go now in the peace of Christ
 to reflect on the Scriptures
 and break open the Word of God in your lives.

Prayer of the faithful:

That our neophytes, those brought into full communion with us at the Easter Vigil, may know peace and joy in their lives, let us pray to the Lord.
 That our candidates and catechumens may experience the guidance of the Holy Spirit as they journey into our faith community, let us pray to the Lord.

Dismissal based on John 14:23-29.

Seventh Sunday of Easter (C)

[After the proclamation of the gospel or after the homily, the presider says:]

> **Would our candidates and catechumens please come forward?**

[When they have reached the dismissal area, he walks over to them and dismisses them with these words:]

> **My dear candidates and catechumens,**
> > **as Christians we are called to a oneness in Jesus—**
> > > **his life maturing in each of us.**
> > **In today's gospel**
> > > **Jesus prays that our oneness may be complete.**
> > > > **This is a life-long task**
> > > > > **because it is a call to oneness**
> > > > > **with all our sisters and brothers.**
> > **May you be willing to nurture this oneness**
> > > **with others and thus grow into the likeness of Christ**
> > > > **by your attitudes, your words, and your actions.**
>
> > **Go now in the peace of Christ**
> > > **to reflect on the Scriptures**
> > > > **and break open the Word of God in your lives.**

Prayer of the faithful:

> **That our neophytes, those brought into full communion with us at the Easter Vigil, may continue to grow in their oneness in Christ, let us pray to the Lord.**
> **That our candidates and catechumens may strongly desire a oneness in the Lord, let us pray to the Lord.**

Dismissal based on John 17:20-26.

Pentecost (C)

[After the proclamation of the gospel or after the homily, the presider says:]

Would our candidates and catechumens please come forward?

[When they have reached the dismissal area, he walks over to them and dismisses them with these words:]

My dear candidates and catechumens,
like the disciples,
we are gathered together as a community in prayer.
Even closed doors and fearful hearts
do not hinder God's Spirit from reaching us.
May each of you experience the Spirit of the Lord
working in your lives
as you reflect on today's Scriptures.

Go now in the peace of Christ,
that peace which he gives each of you
and be nourished by the Word of God.
We look forward to the day when you will join with us
at the Eucharistic table.

Prayer of the faithful:

For our neophytes, that they may experience the Holy Spirit working in their lives and calling them to ministry, let us pray to the Lord.
That the Holy Spirit may continue to guide our candidates and catechumens and fill their hearts with his love, let us pray to the Lord.

Dismissal based on the theme of the feast.

Trinity Sunday (C)

[After the proclamation of the gospel or after the homily, the presider says:]

> **Would our candidates and catechumens please come forward?**

[When they have reached the dismissal area, he walks over to them and dismisses them with these words:]

> **My dear candidates and catechumens,**
> **in our celebration of Trinity Sunday today,**
> **we pray that God the Father, God the Son,**
> **and God the Holy Spirit be revealed to you.**
>
> **May the God of tenderness, the God of compassion,**
> **and the God of love and faithfulness,**
> **touch each of your lives.**
>
> **May you always be open to the mystery**
> **of the presence and love of the Triune God,**
> **as you continue your journey of faith**
> **into full communion with this community.**
>
> **Go now in the peace of Christ,**
> **and be nourished by the Word of God.**
> **We look forward to the day when you will join us**
> **to be nourished at the Eucharistic table.**

Prayer of the faithful:

> **For our candidates and catechumens, that they may be ever open to the mystery of the presence and love of the Triune God in their lives, let us pray to the Lord.**

Dismissal based on the theme of the feast.

The Body and Blood of Christ (C)

[After the proclamation of the gospel or after the homily, the presider says:]

Would our candidates and catechumens please come forward?

[When they have reached the dismissal area, he walks over to them and dismisses them with these words:]

My dear candidates and catechumens,
today we celebrate the reality
that the Lord Jesus gave himself to us
under the form of bread and wine.

May each of you grow in a realization of the
real presence
of the Lord in the Eucharist,
and come to a better understanding
that in the Eucharist
we are united to the Lord Jesus,
and to one another.

Go now in the peace of Christ
to be nourished by the Word of God.
We look forward to the day when you will join
with us
and be nourished by Jesus himself in the Eucharist.

Prayer of the faithful:

That our candidates and catechumens may grow in an appreciation for the sacrament of the Eucharist, let us pray to the Lord.

Dismissal based on John 6:51-58.

Second Sunday of Ordinary Time (C)

[After the proclamation of the gospel or after the homily, the presider says:]

> Would our candidates and catechumens please come forward?

[When they have reached the dismissal area, he walks over to them and dismisses them with these words:]

> My dear candidates and catechumens,
>> a new name, gifts, and a celebration
>>> will be fulfilled in a very special way
>>> for you this year!
>> Each of you will receive a new name,
>>> either in your baptism or your confirmation.
>> Each of you will be asked to look at your gifts
>>> and to consider sharing them with this,
>>> your faith community.
>> Each of you will enter the celebration
>>> of a full sacramental life in this faith community.
>
>> Go now to reflect on these readings
>>> and how they touch your life.
>> We look forward to the day when we will experience
>>> these readings become a reality for you.

Prayer of the faithful:

> That our candidates and catechumens may deepen their faith in the transforming love of our God, let us pray to the Lord.

Dismissal based on Isa 62:1-5; 1 Cor 12:4-11; John 2:1-12.

Third Sunday of Ordinary Time (C)

[After the proclamation of the gospel or after the homily, the presider says:]

> Would our candidates and catechumens please come forward?

[When they have reached the dismissal area, he walks over to them and dismisses them with these words:]

> My dear candidates and catechumens,
>> our readings today remind all of us
>>> of the importance of listening to the Word of God,
>>>> for it is in the hearing of his Word
>>>> that God speaks to us.
>> Let us be aware that ours is the challenge
>>> to be open to the Scriptures,
>>> to respond to that Word,
>>> and seek ways to apply it in our lives.
> My dear friends, that is what this stage
>> of the catechumenate is all about.
>
> Go now in the peace of Christ
>> to reflect on the Scriptures
>> and break open the Word of God in your lives.

Prayer of the faithful:

> That our candidates and catechumens may find
> nourishment for their lives as they continue to reflect
> on the Scriptures each Sunday, let us pray to the Lord.

Dismissal based on Neh 8:2-4, 5-6, 8-10; Luke 1:1-4; 4:14-21.

Fourth Sunday of Ordinary Time (C)

[After the proclamation of the gospel or after the homily, the presider says:]

Would our candidates and catechumens please come forward?

[When they have reached the dismissal area, he walks over to them and dismisses them with these words:]

My dear candidates and catechumens,
if Jesus is rejected by some,
we, his followers cannot expect
that it will be any different for us.
You have made a decision to join with us
in our Catholic faith tradition.
Your decision may have cost you:
perhaps someone does not understand why;
perhaps someone has rejected you
because of your decision.
My dear friends, it isn't easy to be a Catholic,
and if some of us think it is,
then I must question how fully we are living
our Catholic faith.

Go now in the peace of Christ
to reflect on the Scriptures
and break open the Word of God in your lives.

Prayer of the faithful:

That our candidates and catechumens will remain
strong in their desire to follow Jesus, no matter what
criticism they may receive, let us pray to the Lord.

Dismissal based on Luke 4:21-30.

Fifth Sunday of Ordinary Time (C)

[After the proclamation of the gospel or after the homily, the presider says:]

Would our candidates and catechumens please come forward?

[When they have reached the dismissal area, he walks over to them and dismisses them with these words:]

My dear candidates and catechumens,
the Scripture readings for today describe God's call:
he calls Isaiah, he calls Paul,
he calls out to Peter.
We believe that the Lord has also called each of you;
he has asked you to go out into deep waters.
What does this mean for your life?
Know that you have our prayerful support as you
venture out
to answer the Lord's call.

Go now in the peace of Christ
to be nourished on the Word of God.
We look forward to the day when you will be called
to the Eucharistic table.

Prayer of the faithful:

That our candidates and catechumens will be
courageous and generous in following the call of the
Lord, let us pray to the Lord.

Dismissal based on Isa 6:1-2, 3-8; 1 Cor 15:1-11; Luke 5:1-11.

Sixth Sunday of Ordinary Time (C)

[After the proclamation of the gospel or after the homily, the presider says:]

> Would our candidates and catechumens please come forward?

[When they have reached the dismissal area, he walks over to them and dismisses them with these words:]

> My dear candidates and catechumens,
> the Scripture readings for today encourage each of us
> to put our trust in God—
> a trust that goes beyond the boundaries
> of the here and now.
> There is also a challenge in the readings
> that I encourage each of you to take seriously:
> we are asked to take a long hard look
> at what we really value in life.
>
> Go now in the peace of Christ
> to reflect on the Scriptures
> and break open the Word of God in your lives.

Prayer of the faithful:

> That our candidates and catechumens will sincerely
> reevaluate what they value in life in the light of
> today's Scriptures, let us pray to the Lord.

Dismissal based on Jer 17:5-8; 1 Cor 15:12, 16-20; Luke 6:17, 20-26.

Seventh Sunday of Ordinary Time (C)

[After the proclamation of the gospel or after the homily, the presider says:]

> Would our candidates and catechumens please come forward?

[When they have reached the dismissal area, he walks over to them and dismisses them with these words:]

> My dear candidates and catechumens,
>   the gospel reading for today surely speaks to our lives
>   and challenges each of us here present.
> The call to grow in our likeness to Christ:
>   to respond lovingly
>   when faced with the destructive acts of others,
>   to take the initiative
>   of caring and forgiving,
>   this is our constant call to Christian maturity.
>
> May each of you hold the gospel up as a mirror
>   to your life;
>   reflect on it and hear its challenge.
>
> Go now in the peace of Christ
>   to ponder these Scriptures
>   and break open the Word of God in your lives.

Prayer of the faithful:

> That our candidates and catechumens may accept the challenge of today's gospel and thus grow in the likeness of Christ, let us pray to the Lord.

Dismissal based on Luke 6:27-38.

Eighth Sunday of Ordinary Time (C)

[After the proclamation of the gospel or after the homily, the presider says:]

> **Would our candidates and catechumens please come forward?**

[When they have reached the dismissal area, he walks over to them and dismisses them with these words:]

> **My dear candidates and catechumens,**
>> **there is no getting around today's readings.**
>>> **We are all called upon to bear good fruit!**
>> **And so today I ask each of you**
>>> **to reflect on the fruits that you are developing.**
>> **How has the love and example of Christ**
>>> **been an inspiration to you?**
>> **How has his life born fruit in yours?**
>
> **Go now in the peace of Christ**
>> **to be nourished by the Word of God**
>> **and to examine what fruits your life is bearing.**
>> **We look forward to the day when you will join with us**
>>> **to be nourished at the Eucharistic table.**

Prayer of the faithful:

> **That our candidates and catechumens may seriously consider if their lives are bearing good fruit, let us pray to the Lord.**

Dismissal based on Sir 27:4-7; Luke 6:39-45.

Ninth Sunday of Ordinary Time (C)

[After the proclamation of the gospel or after the homily, the presider says:]

> Would our candidates and catechumens please come forward?

[When they have reached the dismissal area, he walks over to them and dismisses them with these words:]

> My dear candidates and catechumens,
>   in the Scripture readings for today
>   we have heard of Jesus' power to heal.
> May each of you become more and more aware
>   of his healing presence in your lives
>   and be open to his touch as you journey
>   into the sacramental life of your Catholic faith.
>
> Go now in the peace of Christ
>   to be nourished on the Scriptures
>   and break open the Word of God in your lives.

Prayer of the faithful:

> That our candidates and catechumens may experience the healing power of Christ in their lives, let us pray to the Lord.

Dismissal based on Luke 7:1-10.

Tenth Sunday of Ordinary Time (C)

[After the proclamation of the gospel or after the homily, the presider says:]

> **Would our candidates and catechumens please come forward?**

[When they have reached the dismissal area, he walks over to them and dismisses them with these words:]

> **My dear candidates and catechumens,**
>   **today's Scriptures present us with accounts**
>   **of God's compassion: both widows have their sons**
>   **restored to them.**
>   **It is in Christ Jesus that we can see**
>   **the fullness of God's compassion.**
>   **The Lord's hand is also outstretched**
>   **into the depths of our brokenness**
>   **to bring each of us to wholeness.**
>   **May each of you experience his compassion**
>   **and in that encounter extend that same compassion**
>   **to others.**
>
> **Go now in the peace of Christ**
>   **to reflect on the Scriptures**
>   **and be people of compassion.**

Prayer of the faithful:

> **That our candidates and catechumens may be people**
> **of compassion, let us pray to the Lord.**

Dismissal based on 1 Kgs 17:17-24; Luke 7:11-17.

Eleventh Sunday of Ordinary Time (C)

[After the proclamation of the gospel or after the homily, the presider says:]

Would our candidates and catechumens please come forward?

[When they have reached the dismissal area, he walks over to them and dismisses them with these words:]

> **My dear candidates and catechumens,**
> **the Scripture readings which we have all**
> **listened to this morning,**
> **confront us with the reality**
> **that one of the primary values of the Christian**
> **is to forgive.**
> **May your reflections this morning lead you to consider**
> **how Jesus may desire to manifest his forgiveness**
> **through you.**
>
> **Go now in the peace of Christ**
> **to reflect on the Scriptures**
> **and break open the Word of God in your lives.**

Prayer of the faithful:

> **That our candidates and catechumens may have the courage to accept Christ's forgiveness and extend that same forgiveness and peace to others, let us pray to the Lord.**

Dismissal based on 2 Sam 12:7-10, 13; Luke 7:36–8:3.

Twelfth Sunday of Ordinary Time (C)

[After the proclamation of the gospel or after the homily, the presider says:]

> **Would our candidates and catechumens please come forward?**

[When they have reached the dismissal area, he walks over to them and dismisses them with these words:]

> **My dear candidates and catechumens,**
>> **the Scriptures proclaimed in our midst this morning**
>>> **challenge all of us to answer**
>>>> **who Christ is for us**
>>>> **and how we are following in his steps.**
>
> **May your reflections on these Scriptures**
>> **help each of you as you journey**
>> **into the fullness of our Catholic faith tradition.**
>
> **Go now in the peace of Christ**
>> **to be nourished by the Word of God.**
>> **We look forward to the day when you will join us**
>>> **to be nourished at the Eucharistic table.**

Prayer of the faithful:

> **That our candidates and catechumens may seriously reflect on who Jesus is for them, and live as his followers, let us pray to the Lord.**

Dismissal based on Luke 9:18-24.

Thirteenth Sunday of Ordinary Time (C)

[After the proclamation of the gospel or after the homily, the presider says:]

> Would our candidates and catechumens please come forward?

[When they have reached the dismissal area, he walks over to them and dismisses them with these words:]

> My dear candidates and catechumens,
>   messages of both freedom and commitment
>   are found in today's readings.
> May your reflections on the Word of God
>   lay bare any areas of your life
>   where you are not yet free,
>   as well as those areas of your life
>   where you feel challenged
>   to commit yourself more fully to the Lord.
>
> Go now in the peace of Christ
>   to reflect on the Scriptures
>   and break open the Word of God in your lives.

Prayer of the faithful:

> That our candidates and catechumens may experience freedom in their choices as they commit their lives to Jesus in our Catholic faith tradition, let us pray to the Lord.

Dismissal based on 1 Kgs 19:16, 19-21; Gal 5:1, 13-18; Luke 9:51-62.

Fourteenth Sunday of Ordinary Time (C)

[After the proclamation of the gospel or after the homily, the presider says:]

Would our candidates and catechumens please come forward?

[When they have reached the dismissal area, he walks over to them and dismisses them with these words:]

My dear candidates and catechumens,
this morning our Scriptures confront us with the fact
that we, too, are called and empowered
by our baptism to be disciples of Jesus.

May your reflections on these readings
help you become more aware
of those places in your lives and in our world
where God's power is active.

Go now in the peace of Christ,
be nourished and be strengthened ✛
to live as a disciple of Jesus
in all the demands of this week.

Prayer of the faithful:

That our candidates and catechumens may become
more aware of those places in their lives where God's
power is active, let us pray to the Lord.

Dismissal based on Gal 6:14-18; Luke 10:1-12, 17-20.

Fifteenth Sunday of Ordinary Time (C)

[After the proclamation of the gospel or after the homily, the presider says:]

> **Would our candidates and catechumens please come forward?**

[When they have reached the dismissal area, he walks over to them and dismisses them with these words:]

> **My dear candidates and catechumens,**
> > **sometimes God's love manifests itself in unexpected ways.**
> **May the Word of God, proclaimed in our assembly today,**
> > **challenge you to love our God totally,**
> > > **with your total heart, soul, strength, mind,**
> > > **and your very self.**
>
> **Go now in the peace of Christ**
> > **to reflect on and be nourished by the Scriptures.**
> **Make a special effort to live the Word of God**
> > **by sharing your love with all those**
> > **you meet this week.**

Prayer of the faithful:

> **That our candidates and catechumens, along with all our parish family, may grow in an understanding that everlasting life is ours—if we are willing to take the risk of sharing our love, let us pray to the Lord.**

Dismissal based on Deut 30:10-14; Luke 10:25-37.

Sixteenth Sunday of Ordinary Time (C)

[After the proclamation of the gospel or after the homily, the presider says:]

> **Would our candidates and catechumens please come forward?**

[When they have reached the dismissal area, he walks over to them and dismisses them with these words:]

> **My dear candidates and catechumens,**
> **our Scripture readings for this Sunday**
> **speak to us of hospitality**
> **and the blessings given to those who offer it.**
>
> **May your openness and presence to all you meet this week**
> **reveal God's presence in you**
> **and touch the lives of others**
> **with his care and concern.**
>
> **Go now in the peace of Christ,**
> **to reflect on the Scriptures**
> **and break open the Word of God in your lives.**

Prayer of the faithful:

> **That our candidates and catechumens may experience hospitality here in our parish family, let us pray to the Lord.**

Dismissal based on Gen 18:1-10; Luke 10:38-42.

Seventeenth Sunday of Ordinary Time (C)

[After the proclamation of the gospel or after the homily, the presider says:]

> Would our candidates and catechumens please come forward?

[When they have reached the dismissal area, he walks over to them and dismisses them with these words:]

> My dear candidates and catechumens,
>> today's Scripture readings remind us
>>> of the importance of prayer in our lives.
>> In prayer may you continue to offer God
>>> your very self, holding nothing back.
>>> For then, my dear friends,
>>>> you will come to know God's love for you
>>>>> and come to discover how safe you are
>>>>> in his loving embrace.
>> Take time out in your busy lives this week
>>> to allow God to love you.
>>> For that is what prayer is:
>>>> allowing God to love us!
>
>> Go now in the peace of Christ
>>> to reflect on the Scriptures
>>> and break open the Word of God in your lives.

Prayer of the faithful:

> That our candidates and catechumens may give themselves entirely to God in prayer and experience his loving embrace, let us pray to the Lord.

Dismissal based on Gen 18:20-32; Luke 11:1-13.

Eighteenth Sunday of Ordinary Time (C)

[After the proclamation of the gospel or after the homily, the presider says:]

Would our candidates and catechumens please come forward?

[When they have reached the dismissal area, he walks over to them and dismisses them with these words:]

My dear candidates and catechumens,
we have all been challenged this morning
by the Scripture readings.
As you reflect on these Scriptures
may you get in touch with your attitude
toward possessions.
We pray that you realize that need we all have
of making God, rather than things,
the center of our lives.

Go now in the peace of Christ
to be nourished on the Word of God.
We look forward to the day when you will join us
to be nourished at the Eucharistic table.

Prayer of the faithful:

That our candidates and catechumens may grow in the realization that their relationship with God is what is of primary importance in the life of a Christian, let us pray to the Lord.

Dismissal based on Eccl 1:2; 2:21-23; Col 3:1-5, 9-11; Luke 12:13-21.

Nineteenth Sunday of Ordinary Time (C)

[After the proclamation of the gospel or after the homily, the presider says:]

Would our candidates and catechumens please come forward?

[When they have reached the dismissal area, he walks over to them and dismisses them with these words:]

My dear candidates and catechumens,
today's Scripture readings remind us
that life is a journey,
and that journey needs to be lived with awareness.
As you journey with this faith community
we pray that you are growing in your awareness
of God's faithfulness to you.

May you grow in consciousness that there is meaning to your lives.

Go now in the peace of Christ
to reflect on the Scriptures
and break open their meaning in your lives.

Prayer of the faithful:

That we, along with our candidates and catechumens, may realize that there is meaning to our lives, let us pray to the Lord.

Dismissal based on Wis 18:6-9; Heb 11:1-2, 8-19; Luke 12:32-48.

Twentieth Sunday of Ordinary Time (C)

[After the proclamation of the gospel or after the homily, the presider says:]

Would our candidates and catechumens please come forward?

[When they have reached the dismissal area, he walks over to them and dismisses them with these words:]

My dear candidates and catechumens,
today's gospel calls for a way of life
that often stands in contradiction
to our materialistic culture.
As Americans it seems that we must have
two or three of everything;
and what we do possess
ends up becoming our identity.
In contrast, my friends, your identity
is that of the *Christian*.

May you accept and heed the challenge Jesus offers,
knowing that he gives you the strength and courage
to make his values your own.

Go now in the peace of Christ
to reflect on the Scriptures
and break open the Word of God in your lives.

Prayer of the faithful:

That our candidates and catechumens may be open to the changes Jesus would have them make in their lives, so that his values become more their own, let us pray to the Lord.

Dismissal based on Heb 12:1-4; Luke 12:49-53.

Twenty-First Sunday of Ordinary Time (C)

[After the proclamation of the gospel or after the homily, the presider says:]

Would our candidates and catechumens please come forward?

[When they have reached the dismissal area, he walks over to them and dismisses them with these words:]

My dear candidates and catechumens,
today's Scriptures remind us
that the cross is a part of our life journey.
As Christians, we have a distinct perspective
about the cross,
for we understand that through our trials
we have an opportunity
to grow in the likeness of Christ.
May you have the wisdom to realize
that often our crosses give us
a true perspective on life.

Go now in the peace of Christ
to reflect on the Scriptures
and break open the Word of God in your lives.

Prayer of the faithful:

That our candidates and catechumens may grow in their understanding that the cross and a constant conversion are integral aspects of our Christian life, let us pray to the Lord.

Dismissal based on Heb 12:5-7, 11-13; Luke 13:22-30.

Twenty-Second Sunday of Ordinary Time (C)

[After the proclamation of the gospel or after the homily, the presider says:]

Would our candidates and catechumens please come forward?

[When they have reached the dismissal area, he walks over to them and dismisses them with these words:]

My dear candidates and catechumens,
  our Scripture readings for today indicate
    that God has a way of accepting the rejects:
      the beggars, the crippled,
      the lame, and the blind.
  May this lead you to consider who are the rejects
    that your life could touch . . .
    and what you are willing to do for them.

Go now in the peace of Christ
  to reflect on the Scriptures
  and break open the Word of God in your lives.

Prayer of the faithful:

That our candidates and catechumens may look at their lives in the light of the gospel message—of a God who accepts the rejects, let us pray to the Lord.

Dismissal based on Luke 14:1, 7-14.

Twenty-Third Sunday of Ordinary Time (C)

[After the proclamation of the gospel or after the homily, the presider says:]

> **Would our candidates and catechumens please come forward?**

[When they have reached the dismissal area, he walks over to them and dismisses them with these words:]

> **My dear candidates and catechumens,**
> **you too are ambassadors for Christ!**
> **May you grow in your awareness, that there are people**
> **who will be part of your life this week,**
> **who may only come to know Jesus**
> **and his love for them**
> **because of the way you touch their lives.**
>
> **Go now and be nourished by the Scriptures.**
> **Consider what it means to you**
> **to be an ambassador for Christ.**
> **We long for the day when you will join us**
> **and be nourished at the Eucharistic table.**

Prayer of the faithful:

> **That our candidates and catechumens may look upon themselves as ambassadors for Christ, let us pray to the Lord.**

Dismissal based on Phlm 9-10, 12-17.

Twenty-Fourth Sunday of Ordinary Time (C)

[After the proclamation of the gospel or after the homily, the presider says:]

> **Would our candidates and catechumens please come forward?**

[When they have reached the dismissal area, he walks over to them and dismisses them with these words:]

> **My dear candidates and catechumens,**
> **Jesus' parables in today's gospel are about each of us.**
> **We can all recognize something of ourselves**
> **in one character or another.**
> **Each parable deals with the idea that**
> **that which is lost is found,**
> **and in that finding there is cause for rejoicing.**
> **May each of you have the humility to recognize**
> **the "lost" in your own lives,**
> **and do what is necessary to restore**
> **any broken relationships.**
>
> **Go now in the peace of Christ**
> **to be nourished by the Scriptures.**
> **We look forward to the day when you will join us**
> **at the Eucharistic banquet.**

Prayer of the faithful:

> **That our candidates and catechumens may have the courage to restore any broken relationships in their lives, let us pray to the Lord.**

Dismissal based on Luke 15:1-32.

Twenty-Fifth Sunday of Ordinary Time (C)

[After the proclamation of the gospel or after the homily, the presider says:]

> **Would our candidates and catechumens please come forward?**

[When they have reached the dismissal area, he walks over to them and dismisses them with these words:]

> **My dear candidates and catechumens,**
> > **we are all called to be honest with ourselves and our God**
> > > **as we acknowledge the gifts**
> > > **that the Lord has given to each of us.**
> > **Now it is up to us to strive to use our gifts**
> > > **in a manner that will further the kingdom.**
> > **May each of you be aware**
> > > **that your talents are God-given,**
> > > **and that they are to be used**
> > > **to touch the lives of others with God's graciousness.**
>
> > **Go now in the peace of Christ**
> > > **to reflect on the Scriptures**
> > > **and break open the Word of God in your lives.**

Prayer of the faithful:

> **That our candidates and catechumens may acknowledge their God-given gifts and be willing to place these gifts at the service of the Christian community, let us pray to the Lord.**

Dismissal based on Luke 16:1-13.

Twenty-Sixth Sunday of Ordinary Time (C)

[After the proclamation of the gospel or after the homily, the presider says:]

> **Would our candidates and catechumens please come forward?**

[When they have reached the dismissal area, he walks over to them and dismisses them with these words:]

> **My dear candidates and catechumens,**
> **today's Scripture readings are a reminder to each of us**
> **of our duty to respond**
> **to the needs of others.**
> **May the acceptance of this truth**
> **engender in each of you a generous spirit**
> **of seeing the needs**
> **of your brothers and sisters in Christ,**
> **and responding to them as you would respond**
> **to Christ himself.**
>
> **Go now in the peace of Christ**
> **to reflect on the meaning of today's Scriptures.**
> **For the truths they contain have the power**
> **to help you advance in spiritual maturity.**

Prayer of the faithful:

> **That our candidates and catechumens may respond to the needs of others with a generous spirit, let us pray to the Lord.**

Dismissal based on Luke 16:19-31.

Twenty-Seventh Sunday of Ordinary Time (C)

[After the proclamation of the gospel or after the homily, the presider says:]

Would our candidates and catechumens please come forward?

[When they have reached the dismissal area, he walks over to them and dismisses them with these words:]

My dear candidates and catechumens,
today's Scriptures are once again in the form of a
parable.
Ours is to be a faith like a mustard seed.
Faith, to be truly faith,
is always growing.
For us the growth needs to take place
from the inside of us outwards
into our daily living.

Go now in the peace of Christ
to be nourished by this parable
and the challenge it brings to your way of life.
We look forward to the day when you will join us
to be nourished at the Eucharistic table.

Prayer of the faithful:

That our candidates and catechumens may have the
courage to express their faith in their daily living, let
us pray to the Lord.

Dismissal based on 2 Tim 1:6-8, 13-14; Luke 17:5-10.

Twenty-Eighth Sunday of Ordinary Time (C)

[After the proclamation of the gospel or after the homily, the presider says:]

Would our candidates and catechumens please come forward?

[When they have reached the dismissal area, he walks over to them and dismisses them with these words:]

My dear candidates and catechumens,
God's Word today is indeed good news!
Jesus has compassion on the lepers
and gives salvation to all who trust in him.
Our prayer for you
is that you may also trust in the Lord
so that he, too, can bring each of you to wholeness
as you continue your faith journey with us.

Go now in the peace of Christ
to reflect on the Scriptures
and break open the Word of God in your lives.

Prayer of the faithful:

That our candidates and catechumens may experience the compassion of Jesus in their lives as they continue to journey with us into the fullness of our Catholic faith, let us pray to the Lord.

Dismissal based on Luke 17:11-19.

Twenty-Ninth Sunday of Ordinary Time (C)

[After the proclamation of the gospel or after the homily, the presider says:]

> Would our candidates and catechumens please come forward?

[When they have reached the dismissal area, he walks over to them and dismisses them with these words:]

> My dear candidates and catechumens,
> in today's gospel Jesus encourages us
> to bring our needs to God in prayer.
> His parable of the widow is an encouragement
> to us to pray and not to lose heart—
> for if even the lazy judge
> will finally hear the cry of one in need,
> how much more will a compassionate God
> respond to our needs.
>
> Go now in the peace of Christ
> let the Scriptures be a source of nourishment for you
> as you take a look at your own prayer life.
> We look forward to the day when you will join us
> to be nourished at the Eucharistic table.

Prayer of the faithful:

> That our candidates and catechumens may value time
> spent in prayer and develop a prayer life that will
> sustain them, let us pray to the Lord.

Dismissal based on Luke 18:1-8.

Thirtieth Sunday of Ordinary Time (C)

[After the proclamation of the gospel or after the homily, the presider says:]

Would our candidates and catechumens please come forward?

[When they have reached the dismissal area, he walks over to them and dismisses them with these words:]

**My dear candidates and catechumens,
today our Scripture readings focus
on two keys to the kingdom of God:
true-self knowledge and repentance.
May you recognize
that God knows us for who we really are—
and that it is not by doing, but by being,
that the Word of the Lord
takes root in our daily lives.
This week may each of you
experience the mercy and compassion of the Lord
and extend mercy and compassion to others
instead of judging them.**

**Go now in the peace of Christ
to reflect on the Scriptures
and break open the Word of God in your lives.**

Prayer of the faithful:

**That our candidates and catechumens may experience
the mercy and compassion of the Lord in their lives
and extend that same mercy and compassion to others,
let us pray to the Lord.**

Dismissal based on Sir 35:12-14, 16-18; Luke 18:9-14.

Thirty-First Sunday of Ordinary Time (C)

[After the proclamation of the gospel or after the homily, the presider says:]

Would our candidates and catechumens please come forward?

[When they have reached the dismissal area, he walks over to them and dismisses them with these words:]

My dear candidates and catechumens,
may you open your hearts to the message of God's
Word today.
Each of us has a Zacchaeus in our own lives—
that aspect of ourselves
waiting to have a deeply personal encounter
with the Lord Jesus.
May you recognize the Zacchaeus within,
and welcome the Lord into those areas of your lives
where you are most in need of his presence.

Go now in the peace of Christ
to reflect on the Scriptures
and break open the Word of God in your lives.

Prayer of the faithful:

That our candidates and catechumens may continue to seek to have a deep personal relationship with the Lord, let us pray to the Lord.

Dismissal based on Luke 19:1-10.

Thirty-Second Sunday of Ordinary Time (C)

[After the proclamation of the gospel or after the homily, the presider says:]

Would our candidates and catechumens please come forward?

[When they have reached the dismissal area, he walks over to them and dismisses them with these words:]

My dear candidates and catechumens,
this life is often filled with unanswered questions.
Together, as a faith community,
we gather together to support each other
in dealing with aspects of our lives
that seem to have no answers.
Together, with us,
may you continue to place your trust in the Lord
who constantly draws you
into a closer relationship with himself.
May you find in this faith community
a support on your journey.

Go now in the peace of Christ
to reflect on the Scriptures
and break open the Word of God in your lives.

Prayer of the faithful:

That our candidates and catechumens may entrust to the Lord those areas of their lives which are troublesome, let us pray to the Lord.

Dismissal based on 2 Thess 2:16–3:5; Luke 20:27-38.

Thirty-Third Sunday of Ordinary Time (C)

[After the proclamation of the gospel or after the homily, the presider says:]

Would our candidates and catechumens please come forward?

[When they have reached the dismissal area, he walks over to them and dismisses them with these words:]

My dear candidates and catechumens,
we find ourselves in a world
where nothing seems permanent,
where often we are confronted with violence
and the threat of destruction.
These are a reminder to all of us
that we have not here a lasting city.
One thing is certain:
God's love for you
and his will for your sanctification.
May his love for you
and your desire for a deeper relationship with him
be a priority in your life—
for this is what will endure.

Go now in the peace of Christ
to reflect on his Word
and break open the Scriptures in your lives.

Prayer of the faithful:

That our candidates and catechumens may value their relationship with the Lord and seek to develop it, let us pray to the Lord.

Dismissal based on Mal 3:19-20; Luke 21:5-19.

Feast of Christ the King (C)

[After the proclamation of the gospel or after the homily, the presider says:]

Would our candidates and catechumens please come forward?

[When they have reached the dismissal area, he walks over to them and dismisses them with these words:]

My dear candidates and catechumens,
  it is not often that Americans
    think of kings and kingdoms.
  However, the kingdom of God is a reality—
    a reality that we pray
      becomes present in our midst each time
      we pray the Our Father.
  Making that kingdom more present on this earth
    is a challenge which each of us faces.
  I encourage you to reflect
    on how you are making the kingdom of God
    more evident in your day-to-day living.

Go now in the peace of Christ
  to reflect on his kingdom
  and the challenge of his Word in your lives.

Prayer of the faithful:

That our candidates and catechumens may realize their responsibility in making the values of the kingdom evident in their daily living, let us pray to the Lord.

Dismissal based on the theme of the feast.

Appendix

This section contains dismissals for Holy Days of Obligation and major feasts which may replace any given Sunday when they occur on a Sunday. The dismissal is the same for each cycle.

February 2—Presentation

[After the proclamation of the gospel or after the homily, the presider says:]

Would our candidates and catechumens please come forward?

[When they have reached the dismissal area, he walks over to them and dismisses them with these words:]

My dear candidates and catechumens,
the Scripture readings for today's feast of the
Presentation
remind us of Jesus' humanity—
how he became like us so that each of us
might be more like him.
The readings also introduce us to Anna and Simeon,
as examples of faith:
Simeon waited in hope
and Anna recognized the child with gratitude.
May each of you, like Simeon and Anna,
experience in Jesus the fulfillment of your hopes
and give gratitude to God.

Go now in the peace of Christ
to reflect on the Scriptures
and the meaning of today's feast in your lives.

Prayer of the faithful:

That our candidates and catechumens may experience in Jesus the fulfillment of their hopes and give thanks to God, let us pray to the Lord.

Dismissal based on the theme of the feast.

March 19—St. Joseph

[After the proclamation of the gospel or after the homily, the presider says:]

> Would our candidates and catechumens please come forward?

[When they have reached the dismissal area, he walks over to them and dismisses them with these words:]

> My dear candidates and catechumens,
>   scripturally we know little about Saint Joseph,
>   whose feast we celebrate today.
>   But all that we know is good!
> His was an unusual position,
>   to care and provide for the Son of God
>   and his Mother, Mary.
> Through the intercession of Joseph,
>   may each of you be faithful to your calling in life.
>
> Go now in the peace of Christ
>   to reflect on the Scriptures
>   and the meaning of today's feast to you.

Prayer of the faithful:

> That our candidates and catechumens may find in Saint Joseph an example of fidelity and loving care, let us pray to the Lord.

Dismissal based on the theme of the feast.

March 25—Annunciation

[After the proclamation of the gospel or after the homily, the presider says:]

> Would our candidates and catechumens please come forward?

[When they have reached the dismissal area, he walks over to them and dismisses them with these words:]

> My dear candidates and catechumens,
>   today our liturgy focuses upon Mary,
>   who does not understand, but accepts
>   that nothing is impossible with God.
> May each of you grow in the realization
>   that relying on God and his love for you,
>   you will be able to face all the events of your lives.
>
> Go now in the peace of Christ
>   to reflect on the Scriptures
>   and the meaning of the feast of the Annunciation
>   in your lives.

Prayer of the faithful:

> That our candidates and catechumens may rely on God during troubling times of their lives, let us pray to the Lord.

Dismissal based on the theme of the feast.

June 24—Birth of John the Baptist

[After the proclamation of the gospel or after the homily, the presider says:]

Would our candidates and catechumens please come forward?

[When they have reached the dismissal area, he walks over to them and dismisses them with these words:]

My dear candidates and catechumens,
today we celebrate the birth of Saint John the Baptist
whose mission in life was
to call people to conversion,
to announce that our God is a compassionate God,
and to point Christ out to others.
The very name "John" means "God is graceful."
Through the intercession of John the Baptist,
may you also see the areas of your lives
that are in need of conversion
and have the courage to change.
Then you, too, will experience that "God is graceful."

Go now in the peace of Christ
to reflect on the Scriptures
and the meaning of this feast for your lives.

Prayer of the faithful:

That our candidates and catechumens may grow in an awareness that God is a God of compassion and love, let us pray to the Lord.

Dismissal based on the theme of the feast.

June 29—Saints Peter and Paul

[After the proclamation of the gospel or after the homily, the presider says:]

Would our candidates and catechumens please come forward?

[When they have reached the dismissal area, he walks over to them and dismisses them with these words:]

My dear candidates and catechumens,
   today we celebrate the feast of two men
      who believed in Jesus so much
      that they spread their faith in him
         throughout the Mediterranean world.
   Both men suffered and died because of their belief
      that Jesus is Lord.
   May Saint Peter and Saint Paul be an inspiration to you
      to live what you believe
      and to share your beliefs with others,
         both by what you say and what you do.

Go now in the peace of Christ
   to be nourished by the Scriptures
   and ponder the meaning of this feast in your lives.

Prayer of the faithful:

That the faith that our candidates and catechumens
have in Jesus may bear fruit in their lives, let us pray
to the Lord.

Dismissal based on the theme of the feast.

August 6—Transfiguration

[After the proclamation of the gospel or after the homily, the presider says:]

Would our candidates and catechumens please come forward?

[When they have reached the dismissal area, he walks over to them and dismisses them with these words:]

My dear candidates and catechumens,
    there are those moments in each of our lives
        when we have a glimpse of what God is truly like.
His is the power to transform the situations
        in our lives
    most needing his presence.
May you be open to his transforming power
        in your lives
    as you continue your faith journey
        into the Catholic community.

Go now in the peace of Christ
    to be nourished by the Scriptures
    and to ponder the meaning of this feast in your lives.

Prayer of the faithful:

That our candidates and catechumens may be open to the transforming power of God in their lives, let us pray to the Lord.

Dismissal based on the theme of the feast.

August 15—Assumption

[After the proclamation of the gospel or after the homily, the presider says:]

> **Would our candidates and catechumens please come forward?**

[When they have reached the dismissal area, he walks over to them and dismisses them with these words:]

> **My dear candidates and catechumens,**
> **today we celebrate the Assumption of Mary,**
> **her victory, through the merits of her Son, over death.**
>
> **Each feast of Mary that we Catholics commemorate,**
> **really points to something about ourselves.**
> **Today we recall that like Mary, we too,**
> **are destined for eternal life.**
> **That is why we celebrate this feast!**
> **May Mary help each of you to always be open**
> **to the Word of God as you continue**
> **your journey with us.**
>
> **Go now in the peace of Christ**
> **to be nourished by the Scriptures**
> **and to ponder the meaning of this feast in your lives.**

Prayer of the faithful:

> **That through the intercession of Mary, our candidates and catechumens may realize that they are destined for eternal life, let us pray to the Lord.**

Dismissal based on the theme of the feast.

September 14—Triumph of the Cross

[After the proclamation of the gospel or after the homily, the presider says:]

Would our candidates and catechumens please come forward?

[When they have reached the dismissal area, he walks over to them and dismisses them with these words:]

My dear candidates and catechumens,
in today's feast we celebrate the fact
that it was on a cross, an instrument of execution,
that Jesus overcame all evil.
Because of this, the symbol of a cross no longer
represents just a shameful way to die.
Instead, it speaks to us now of blessing,
of redemption, and of salvation.
May the cross that you wear
not be a decoration for you,
but a declaration of the fact
that you belong to Christ.

Go now in the peace of Christ
to be nourished by the Scriptures
and to ponder the meaning of this feast in your lives.

Prayer of the faithful:

That our candidates and catechumens may find
meaning in the cross of Christ, let us pray to the Lord.

Dismissal based on the theme of the feast.

November 1—All Saints

[After the proclamation of the gospel or after the homily, the presider says:]

> Would our candidates and catechumens please come forward?

[When they have reached the dismissal area, he walks over to them and dismisses them with these words:]

> My dear candidates and catechumens,
> the beauty of today, the feast of All Saints,
>   is that it enables us to recognize
>   the many people whose lives have reflected
>   the spirit of the beatitudes.
> Our saints are important to us
>   because they show us how real people,
>   in real life situations,
>   have put Jesus' teachings into practice.
> May you understand that you, too,
>   are called to holiness,
>   called to make Jesus' teachings evident
>   in your own lives.
>
> Go now in the peace of Christ
>   to reflect on the Scriptures
>   and the meaning of this feast in your lives.

Prayer of the faithful:

> That our candidates and catechumens may realize that they are called to make Jesus' teachings evident in their lives, let us pray to the Lord.

Dismissal based on the theme of the feast.

November 2—All Souls

[After the proclamation of the gospel or after the homily, the presider says:]

Would our candidates and catechumens please come forward?

[When they have reached the dismissal area, he walks over to them and dismisses them with these words:]

**My dear candidates and catechumens,
today we recall all our loved ones
who have gone before us.
We pray that each of them
may now know the loving embrace of the Lord,
who triumphed over death.
Today we also recall that each one of us
will face death.
May your faith in the resurrection
sustain you as you recall your loved ones
who have gone before you.
And may each of you live in such a way
that your lives bear witness
to your belief in eternal life.**

Prayer of the faithful:

That our candidates and catechumens may grow in their understanding of the communion of saints, let us pray to the Lord.

Dismissal based on the theme of the feast.

November 9—Dedication of the Church of Saint John Lateran

[After the proclamation of the gospel or after the homily, the presider says:]

> Would our candidates and catechumens please come forward?

[When they have reached the dismissal area, he walks over to them and dismisses them with these words:]

> My dear candidates and catechumens,
>   today we celebrate the feast of the dedication
>   of our cathedral in Rome,
>   the Church of Saint John Lateran.
> But it is more than the presence of this beautiful building
>   that we celebrate.
> We, as a Catholic community, celebrate our unity
>   with all other Catholics who also share this building
>   as their cathedral in Rome.
> The Church of Saint John Lateran, beautiful as it is,
>   is a reminder that we together are the temple of God.
>   His holiness is destined to dwell in each of us.
>
> Go now in the peace of Christ
>   to be nourished by the Scriptures
>   and ponder the meaning of this feast in your lives.

Prayer of the faithful:

> That our candidates and catechumens may experience the call to holiness that is theirs, let us pray to the Lord.

Dismissal based on the theme of the feast.

December 8—Immaculate Conception

[After the proclamation of the gospel or after the homily, the presider says:]

Would our candidates and catechumens please come forward?

[When they have reached the dismissal area, he walks over to them and dismisses them with these words:]

My dear candidates and catechumens,
today we celebrate the feast of the Immaculate
Conception.
We celebrate the fact that Mary, the Mother of God,
was born free of all sin.
We celebrate that Mary was never controlled by evil.
Each feast of Mary that we Catholics celebrate
really points to something about ourselves.
Today we recall that like Mary, we too,
through her Son's redemptive love
have power over evil by our baptism.
May you resist the power of evil
when it entices you to sin.
May Mary, your Mother, assist you to live
in touch with God's presence.

Go now in the peace of Christ
to be nourished by the Scriptures
and to ponder the meaning of this feast in your lives.

Prayer of the faithful:

That our candidates and catechumens may experience
the love and concern of the Mother of God for them,
let us pray to the Lord.

Dismissal based on the theme of the feast.